Still Here with Me

of related interest

Relative Grief
**Parents and Children, Sisters and Brothers, Husbands, Wives
and Partners, Grandparents and Grandchildren Talk about their
Experience of Death and Grieving**
Clare Jenkins and Judy Merry
Foreword by Dorothy Rowe
ISBN-13: 978 1 84310 257 1   ISBN-10: 1 84310 257 9

**Without You – Children and Young People Growing Up
with Loss and its Effects**
Tamar Granot
ISBN-13: 978 1 84310 297 7   ISBN-10: 1 84310 297 8

Children Also Grieve
Talking about Death and Healing
Linda Goldman
ISBN-13: 978 1 84310 808 5   ISBN-10: 1 84310 808 9

Talking with Children and Young People about Death and Dying
A Resource
Second Edition
Mary Turner
Illustrations by Bob Thomas
ISBN-13: 978 1 84310 441 4   ISBN-10: 1 84310 441 5

Someone Very Important Has Just Died
**Immediate Help for People Caring for Children of All Ages at the
Time of a Close Bereavement**
Mary Turner
Illustrated by Elaine Bailey
ISBN-13: 978 1 84310 295 3   ISBN-10: 1 84310 295 1

Lost for Words
Loss and Bereavement Awareness Training
John Holland, Ruth Dance, Nic MacManus and Carole Stitt
ISBN-13: 978 1 84310 324 0   ISBN-10: 1 84310 324 9

Love and Grief
The Dilemma of Facing Love After Death
Catherine O'Neill and Lisa Keane
Foreword by the WAY Foundation
ISBN-13: 978 1 84310 346 2   ISBN-10: 1 84310 346 X

When a Family Pet Dies
A Guide to Dealing with Children's Loss
JoAnn Tuzeo-Jarolmen, Ph.D.
Foreword by Linda Tintle
ISBN-13: 978 1 84310 836 8   ISBN-10: 1 84310 836 4

Still Here with Me

Teenagers and Children on Losing a Parent

Edited by Suzanne Sjöqvist

Translated by Margaret Myers

Jessica Kingsley Publishers
London and Philadelphia

First published in 2005 in Swedish by
Wahlström & Widstrand, Stockholm, Sweden, as *Du är hos mig ändå*

This edition first published in English in 2007
by arrangement with Bonnier Group Agency, Stockholm, Sweden
by Jessica Kingsley Publishers
116 Pentonville Road
London N1 9JB, UK
and
400 Market Street, Suite 400
Philadelphia, PA 19106, USA

www.jkp.com

Library of Congress Cataloging in Publication Data
Du är hos mig ändå. English
    Still here with me : teenagers and children on losing a parent / edited by Suzanne Sjöqvist ; trans-
lated by Margaret Myers.
        p. cm.
    ISBN-13: 978-1-84310-501-5 (pbk.)
    ISBN-10: 1-84310-501-2 (pbk.)
    1. Grief in children. 2. Bereavement in children. 3. Loss (Psychology) in children. 4.
Parents--Death--Psychological aspects. I. Sjöqvist, Suzanne, 1945- II. Title.
    BF723.G75D813 2007
    155.9'37083--dc22

                                                                        2006034313

British Library Cataloguing in Publication Data
A CIP catalogue record for this book is available from the British Library

ISBN-13: 978 1 84310 501 5
ISBN-10: 1 84310 501 2

Printed and bound in the United States by
Thomson-Shore, Inc.

This book is especially for you if you have lost your mum or dad while you are still very young.

Contents

Acknowledgements

I want to give my warmest thanks to all of you who have told me your stories, for your frankness, generosity and matchless cooperation. My thanks also go to your families for their trust and great helpfulness.

Thank you Wahlström & Widstrand and my publisher Stefan Hilding who was the first person to see that a book like this was as important as it was lacking.

Thank you Jessica Kingsley Publishers and Stephen Jones who saw that these stories from faraway Sweden are universal and relevant even out in the big wide world.

Thank you everyone who has the strength to help other people's children and to be significant in their lives. You have shared your time and experience as a matter of course when I have interrupted you in your work. Ken Chesterson and Lars Widén, who have built up a child trauma clinic, Nilofar Shirinbek, a school welfare officer, and the journalist Alexandra Hjelm. Kristina Ljunggren, a vicar at the Stockholm Cathedral and my partner in discussion. The author Peter Olesen, and Signe Rølmer, a schoolgirl who gave me the idea of a book by children on grief. Elisabeth Pettersson, a hospital chaplain, Charlotta Lindgren and Krister Petterson, funeral directors. Lotta Polfeldt, who has created the Save the Children grief groups. Agneta Bohman, administrator at Save the Children, Maria Schiller, teacher of Swedish, Cecilia Virgin, psychotherapist, Marie Malmgren, bookbinder, Anna Kiesow, emergency nurse, Astrid Hasselrot, author, and Louise Kritschewsky, music teacher. My relatives Peter Oscarsson and Richard Öhman. My colleagues and close friends Monika Björk, Maria-Pia Böethius, Christina Ollén, Margareta Schwartz and Karin Öhlander. Another person who has helped me I only know as Barbro.

Nike Hjelm, a young librarian who lost her father when she was 15, has provided me with gentle criticism and sensitive solutions.

I want to thank my son, my daughters and my husband. You have encouraged me, listened patiently and given me the best possible feedback.

I want to thank Margaret Myers, our translator. She felt that this book was also needed in English to reach and help even more people. Her sensitive translation allows each young person to speak in his or her own tone of voice.

Working with you all has been a true pleasure.

Preface

This is a book by teenagers and children who have lost their mother or father and who all know in the depths of their souls what grief feels like. They write about their darkest hour, about loss and about getting their lives back on track again. They express their thoughts and feelings, and want to share them with other young people who are going through loss and grief, and with us all.

Those of us who lost a parent through death when we were young belong to a fairly large, growing family. New sisters and brothers join our group every day. Only a tiny hint is needed for us 'siblings in grief' to guess when someone else is in a deep hole. We know how uphill and slippery the way back can be, to happiness and a new life. Just seeing that one is not alone can also soothe and relieve.

The message of this book is simple. To those involved: Don't shut me out. Help me to be brave and go into the sickroom, and don't forget that I have the right to say farewell, even if it's in the mortuary. This is my last chance. Let me take part in making decisions about the funeral and planning how we can get on with our lives. And to everyone around: See me, say something, do something, even if it's only a little thing. Don't turn your back on me.

There is a wall of silence. Is it shyness, misdirected thoughtfulness or indifference? It can make sad people feel lonelier and more left out, and silence can hurt. With due respect to the professionals, it is us amateurs who are still there when crisis counselling is cut back and the support group is discontinued. We are relatives, classmates, boy- and girlfriends, family friends, neighbours, teachers, coaches… We want and are able to give support, but are sometimes hopelessly at a loss. We can be clumsy, tongue-tied, intrusive, and, if the worst comes to the worst, we may even run away.

What can one say, what dare one ask, how should one behave? Answers are offered in this book, by the real experts. These stories tell us how young people who are grieving want, and absolutely don't want, to be treated.

'What about your dad?' 'He's dead.' 'Oh, sorry.' End of conversation. Both parts get embarrassed, although the person without a father wants to shout out loud: 'It isn't your fault. Please ask me more!' Hardly anybody does. Are they afraid of making somebody cry, or do they believe that grief is catching? This book can hopefully give people who meet grieving children in their line of work a few ideas about what they could do better: at the hospital, police station and funeral parlour, in the classroom, at the psychologist's, sports practice, church... But these stories are above all from and to teenagers and children who are searching for a straw to catch at and a way of getting their lives back on track.

The idea for a book on grieving children came from a 14-year-old Danish girl who lost her mother when she was 12. Inspired by her, I invited girls and boys from all over Sweden to write about what they had been through. Although most of these young people are still living in that country, their experiences and awareness offer a global perspective. Some of them also come originally from other countries and even continents. Everywhere in the world there are youngsters having to face up to the death of a parent, and they all have a lot in common.

This is a collection of 31 free and open-hearted stories to help give you strength and lessen the loneliness. The oldest contributor in the book is now 20 and the youngest is just one. Yes, it's true. He saw his daddy die and afterwards he couldn't play or sleep. He was frightened, angry and sad. With his psychologist as 'secretary' he was able to 'write' himself out of his pain.

Isn't there a mountain of books about grief already? There are attractive picture books for small children. In them old people die peacefully and are grieved over by children and grandchildren, but there is next to nothing for older children and teenagers. Sudden death or the long, drawn-out kind that rob children of their mothers and fathers are more difficult to think and write about. Here is an attempt to show that it is possible to talk about this subject openly.

Sons and daughters tell their stories with warmth and directness. Several who saw their parent's life ebb away say that it is better for their mother or father to be anywhere but in 'that broken body'. Many live with the hope that when they have left their lives here on earth, they will find their mother or father again, perhaps somewhere beyond the treetops. Until then, parents who are no longer here have found a home in their children, who in different ways combine love with rebellion when they say: You're still here with me, see.

The contributors' fathers and mothers have seldom 'died peacefully in their sleep', because that is not what happens when young, active parents die. Besides, death always seems sudden and unexpected to children. Nine of them lost a mother or father through cancer, six parents had heart attacks, and in two other cases alcohol was involved. Two parents died of rare, incurable diseases. One father died in a car accident, one was killed in a civil war, one crashed his sportsplane and one was the victim of a parachute disaster. A brother and sister lost both their parents to the tsunami in Thailand in December 2004. Two fathers and one mother took their own lives.

Two mothers were killed at home by their husbands, the children's fathers. This is very rare. We read about it in the newspapers and shudder and that's it. But here are two teenagers who tell us what happened afterwards. They lost their mothers and for many years even their fathers, who received long prison sentences for murder. They also lost their homes. They describe how they live with their pain, struggling to create a new everyday life for themselves and knit together family ties that have been torn apart. They want to contribute because they think it is important for people to know that this can happen. We know how vital it is to be able to talk about things and communicate and it would feel wrong not to include their unusual, scary stories. What is done is done. As the afflicted, we need to tell our story and as readers we must try to take it all in even though it is hard.

We must understand the trust that has been shared with us by all the contributors to this book. Without these stories we would perhaps never learn that in horror, darkness and chaos we can find tiny, half-hidden paths that lead out into sunny clearings, to new faith, and reconciliation.

It is probably a good thing to read and talk about this book with grown-ups at home or at school, or in a group that meets to talk about important things, especially if you are very young.

One 16-year-old boy wanted to write so that when he is a grown-up he can read what he felt and thought when he was 13 and became fatherless. He has noticed that he forgets things. He is afraid of losing his memories and wants to have them in a book.

'Heavy, but good' is what many of the contributors have said when they have completed their story of what has happened and described the parent that they miss. I know, because I belong to the same 'union'.

'Please dear good God', I breathed in a top-secret evening prayer, 'promise that Mummy and Daddy will never die, in any case not before me.' But my father Harald did die when I was ten years old. He had a blood clot in his heart. The last time we saw each other I was a traitor, struggling to get out of his embrace when he wanted to give me a hug. I told myself I would never ever be happy again. I kept that promise more or less until I was 17.

'Did you have fun when your dad died?' a girl in my class asks eagerly on the way to school. Surely she can't possibly have said that! But that's what I hear. From that moment on I hate her name, voice, skirt, dog, handwriting, pasty face and the hill where she lives. We are walking along the path through the woods, the day after the funeral and I hiss: 'My dad…he's alive'.

For me, Daddy isn't dead as long as I don't say it in words. One day I will wake up out of my sleeping-beauty slumber and he will be back at home as usual. 'God, make what's happened unhappen, so that I can have Daddy back again.'

DAD IS DEAD. It took me seven years to admit the fact, and this is how it sometimes sounded when I answered the telephone and somebody who I did not know wanted to speak to Daddy:

(Riiiing)

'Hello!'

'Is your daddy at home?'

'No.'

'Do you know when he'll be back?'

'No.'

'Could you ask him to ring me?'

'No.'

'Then I'll ring a little later.'

'No.'

'Has he gone away?'

'Yes.'

'When is he expected home?'

'Never!'

I bang down the receiver.

My mother, Gertrud, did what she could to thaw me out. But it was only when I was 17 that the ice was broken by my boyfriend, John, who settled the matter when he realised that I was avoiding the word 'dead' by saying to me 'Your dad is DEAD, and so is mine.' Then we talked about our fathers for 19 years.

I think that I can discern that young people nowadays who have lost someone and are grieving are more seen and understood. I hope so, because it is important. It must be done right. Every time somebody looks away, every thoughtless or unsaid word, every lie that is supposed to spare feelings remains etched into the memory – just like the tiniest unexpected expression of sympathy. People one hardly knows can become central in one's life as new confidants. It happened to us when my children – then 11, 12 and 15 years old – lost their father to a heart attack. The same morning, the father of one of their classmates stood in the doorway with a bowl of freshly made rice pudding. The classmate's family had taken the day off. The bowl was put on the table, and the family stayed and hugged us. They listened and were silent. They filled vases, brewed coffee and smiled at us. Even though we were not relatives and had not even had time to become close friends. But the classmate's mother had lost her mother when she was nine and she knew what it's like. The father is Greek, and for him it is the custom to hurry to a grieving household, not to 'offer our sympathy in your grief' but to share in it.

My children, and I myself before them, needed this book. The contributors' families and people whose job it is to help the grieving have searched for it. 'If only I had had it then, to give to so-and-so,' they have sighed, and wished our book project good luck.

The oldest person in our sibling group is almost a hundred. She is a mother who recently lost a son. When she was three her own mother died. She is reading this book at the moment, one chapter every evening, and she has said to me: 'It's strange that these children who have written about their darkest hours are helping me to regain my balance, even though I don't know them. I feel on the same wavelength as them.'

A parson I know often visits schools to talk about grief. Her children lost their father when they were 9 and 11. The schoolchildren tell her stories about many different kinds of death, 'from members of the family to stick insects'. She believes that she can see 'a special extra depth of life experience' in children who have lost a parent early on: wisdom and maturity, perhaps not in every way but in many. Childhood can suddenly come to an end, as can trust. Nothing is familiar or easy any longer. Grief demands more energy and more time than many who have been spared it believe. The strength it can lead to in the long run gets built up slowly. It sprouts up in these stories, touchingly, in all its raw power.

All of us 'insiders' hope that this book will help you in your attempt to understand and find peace.

Suzanne Sjöqvist
stillherewithme@telia.com

Rikard

*'I would never again be able to see his
crooked smile or hear his rumbling laugh.
I've lost a lot of my sense of humour.'*

Rikard was born in 1991.
He has written about losing his father, Kjell, some months earlier.

It is time for me to tell the story about Dad and me. I was born in 1991. Dad was already ill. He had Marfan syndrome. This disease led to Dad becoming handicapped and brain damaged. His movements were very stiff and he limped when he walked. He had personal carers who helped him with cooking, going to the lavatory, hygiene and, well, almost everything. He had to move away from where we lived, because he needed his own flat and he needed a lift. I don't think I really understood what was happening, since I was so little.

Mum met a new guy called Mats. He moved in with us and has lived with us for as long as I can remember. My sister and I call him Macken (I don't know why) but never Dad. I didn't think about it at the time. I used to see Dad once a week as well as at Christmas and it was a pure reflex to call him 'Dad'. I didn't really understand at that time that Dad was my father. But the older I got the more I understood that he was my father and not just some close friend of my mother's. When my younger brother was born, he's really my stepbrother, it took quite a while before I understood that we weren't 100 per cent related. There are still a lot of people who seem a bit hesitant when they see my fair-haired kid brother and my pale skin and dark brown hair.

As the years passed my relationship with Dad got better and better. I started to visit him on my own. On these occasions Dad and I talked much more about important things. Of course we joked and said crazy things to each other. We both had a sense of humour and always found amusing things to say. Dad knew a lot of funny songs and tunes and told stories about the countries that he and Mum had visited before he fell ill. We also did a lot of fun things together. I'll never forget when I visited him and we watched the ice-hockey finals between Sweden and Canada a year or so ago (the result was 2–3). Normally I arrived, had dinner, chatted a little and went home, but that time things weren't as usual. It was more than that. I arrived late and we watched the match together.

I'm quite a humorous type of person who always had a joke or a funny story ready when we met. A joke he specially liked was:

'What kind of salt is that; coarse or fine?'

'Coarse!'

'Fine!'

Dad was terribly good at language and very cultivated. He was one of the few people who understood this joke. It was always interesting to listen to his views on everything that was happening in the world around us. But there was no point in playing Trivial Pursuit or other general knowledge games with him, since he always knew the answers better than the game itself. I could always ring Dad if I needed help with my homework: Swedish, geography or history.

Dad had been a foreign affairs journalist before he fell ill. He had masses of weird stuff from different countries, including a picture of a pig and a monkey with a lot of Chinese signs beside them. The monkey is the animal sign that Dad was born under according to the Chinese calendar. The pig is the animal sign that Mum was born under.

But on my birthday, when I turned 13, one of Dad's carers rang and said that Dad couldn't come and celebrate, because he had been taken into hospital. His blood pressure had gone up. Before that I hadn't really thought about the fact that Dad was so ill that he might die soon. At that point I began to understand how ill he really was.

We celebrated anyway. But afterwards my sister, who is 16, my mother and I went to visit him. He had been given morphine because he was in such pain and was very tired when we arrived, but we talked for a long time anyway. He had a photo of my sister and me that he asked to have put up by his bed.

We visited Dad every day. Sometimes he was in another ward. But he always had the photo of my sister and me with him. Sometimes the ward seemed to be a better one, other times a worse one. His blood pressure went down and they reduced his dose of morphine.

But then one day when I was at school they rang from the office and said that my parents were waiting for me. When I came downstairs Macken and Mum were standing there. They looked very sad. They told me that the hospital had rung and said that his condition had worsened. I don't really know what had happened to Dad, but he was dead. We sat there for only a short while, but it felt like forever. I mostly sat and thought that it couldn't be true and that I would soon wake up out of my nightmare. Even though I had thought about Dad dying ever since he was taken into hospital, it still felt unreal that he had died. The only thing I really asked was what had actually happened when Dad died, because his blood pressure had gone down and the day before I had been so certain that he was going to pull through.

I would never ever be able to see Dad on the steps of our house again. I would never again be able to see his crooked smile or hear his rumbling laugh that could make just about anybody laugh too. The fact is that I've lost a lot of my sense of humour since then.

We went and fetched my sister and then we went to the hospital, where my father's brother, father, mother, sister and cousin were waiting. My sister and mother went in to look at Dad. But I felt that I didn't want to see Dad now that there would no longer be any sound coming from him. I felt that I didn't want to see him when he could no longer smile, laugh or speak. A doctor came and told us a little about what had happened. To tell the truth I didn't listen. I thought more about what my life would be like from that moment on.

I had never told anyone that my father was handicapped (only a few really close friends who had met Dad knew), but now I would no longer be able to avoid telling them about it. If anyone asked about my parents I would now say that I didn't have a father, and then that person would be bound to ask what had happened and I would have to say that my dad had been handicapped and of course that is a bit odd.

The following two days my sister, my mother and I stayed at home. The first day we went out to the nearby countryside (Dad had been a great fan of the football club there). We walked and talked and looked at the view, and Mum told us a lot about Dad before he fell ill.

Pretty soon it was time to think about the funeral. My father's sister, brother and father, Mum, my sister and I had a meeting with the vicar, Olle. He was in charge of the whole funeral. Olle asked if my sister and I would each write a letter that Dad could have with him in the coffin. We both wrote letters. When Olle had read my letter he asked if he could read it at the service and I said that would be alright. Olle asked how we remembered Dad, and Mum helped us since we tripped over our words all the time. My dad's sister's, brother's and father's stories were pretty much alike. Mum's story was different and was mostly about what Dad was like when they met and not about what he was like when he was a child.

Olle also asked stuff like when Dad was born and where he had lived. We also met Krister who worked at the funeral parlour and he was very helpful. He discussed with me and my sister a lot about how we wanted things done. Mum and he gave us a lot of useful advice, but my sister and I had the last word.

It was Krister's idea that I should help to carry the coffin. I thought for a long time about whether I should do it or not. He told me how it had been at a lot of other funerals and that so far nobody had complained. He told us all the details about how long the funeral would be and what would happen at it.

I don't remember anything about the days running up to the funeral, apart from the fact that there was a lot of shopping for black and dark clothes. Macken and I bought everything we needed at Dressmann.

Then it was the day of the funeral. I can't say that I exactly longed for that day. I had been rather scared of what it would be like. Dad's closest relatives (me, Sis, Mum, Macken, Dad's parents, brother and sister) arrived at the church before everybody else. We had to sit in a little room. Olle told us once again what would happen at the funeral. After a while the coffin bearers arrived. They were six of Dad's best friends. I didn't know any of them except one man who Mum had been friends with too.

Carrying the coffin into the church turned out to be harder than we thought. The idea was that you should hold the coffin by wrapping your arm round one of its legs. But Dad was too heavy to be carried on your arm, so the six men had to load the coffin up on to their shoulders. I felt a bit lost as I was so short that I couldn't even reach up to the coffin with my shoulder and was only able to touch it with my hand, which hardly did any good physically.

After the coffin had been put in position there was a last chance to see Dad. My sister and my mum went in, but I didn't want to that time either.

When everyone had taken their seats the vicar started to speak. The church wasn't very big and it was wooden. That meant that the vicar's speech wasn't so echoey or booming. For some reason (I don't know why) that felt good.

He spoke a lot about what Dad had been like and he often turned to my sister and me. He read out the letter I had written. It was only about the joke that Dad liked most (the one about the salt). Then there was music and singing. First of all my dad's brother played a tune that he had played at Mum and Dad's wedding (he was very good on the saxophone). It sounded very beautiful. Then a very gifted woman sang three songs in a row. First a hymn that one of Grandma's relatives had made up, then a hymn that had been sung at my sister's confirmation, and finally she sang 'Bridge Over Troubled Water'. Some people cried during the hymns. Mum cried when Dad's brother played the saxophone tune and I'm sure someone also cried when the woman sang 'Bridge Over Troubled Water'. I didn't cry during any of the songs.

Then it was time to file past the coffin. Everybody took it in turns to walk past and put a flower on it or say a last message before sitting down again. Mum, Sis, Macken and I were the first to get up. Mum and my sister put flowers on the coffin. I looked at the plate with Dad's name on it and said a last farewell. I had still not cried. When everyone had been up we in the family went back into the little room again. Then I fell to pieces. I started crying and continued for a long time. I didn't hear a word of what Olle or anyone else said, I just cried.

After the funeral we went to a restaurant for the funeral food and drink (the other children and I had non-alcoholic drinks). In some way it was a relief now that the funeral was over. Mum, Sis and I sat with Macken at the far end of the restaurant. Right by the entrance there was a photo of Dad. A fine photo from Mum and Dad's wedding. In the photo he is smiling his well-known crooked smile. He looked so happy and it really seemed that he was looking out over his friends who were sitting together at one of his favourite restaurants, talking happily and laughing at things they remembered about Dad.

It was just impossible to be unhappy around Dad. Some of his friends gave speeches about the best things they remembered about him.

I thought of giving a speech. I kept on changing my mind: should I or shouldn't I? In the end I decided to do it. My speech went roughly like this:

'Um, hi! You've talked about your friend Kjell, but I want to talk about my dad Kjell! The rest of you knew Dad much longer than I did, and I never knew Dad when he was well. But we were friends too, though in a different way. Dad and I never had rows. We did a lot of things together like going to the cinema or a match. The only thing we sometimes quarrelled about was Dad's allergy to cats. I love those animals but Dad said time and again that the brutes should be flushed down the drain.'

There were a lot of laughs and applause when I finished my speech.

Now I've told the whole story about Dad and me. Life carries on, despite the fact that I often have great difficulty in concentrating on what I have to do and often have to stop and take a break when I know that I shouldn't. But I feel that I have to rest between tasks because otherwise it all gets too much.

Everyone in our family got incredibly tired the days after the death and the funeral. I don't know if it was because we lay and thought about things at night so that we couldn't sleep.

I sometimes feel very sad that Dad and I never got to do all the things we talked about. For example we had planned to see the 'Lord of the Rings' films together so that I could explain them to him (after all I had seen them three times already). That never happened. But despite all the tiredness, all the crying and all the promises that were never kept, it feels like a good thing anyway that it happened at last.

Dad had been ill since the time I was born. In a way it was as though he held on to life just to see what happened to us. But after those 13 years he couldn't hold on any longer. I just hope he is having a better time now.

Rikard

Ida

*'We only had 14 days together. I never
really had a chance to be her daughter.'*

Ida was born in 1985.
She was a newborn baby when she lost her mother, Eva.

It is hard to speak about someone who has died. At least that's what I've always thought. A bit taboo. When I was a small child I felt almost ashamed when Dad started talking about Mum. It got far too emotional. And I didn't want to talk about her with my stepmother, who I felt guilty towards because I would rather have had my real mother. If she had lived it would have meant that my stepmother did not exist in my life.

It took several months before my boyfriend asked about Mum and that is not unusual. Lots of people find it difficult to ask how and when she died. I think it is because they do not want to stir up my feelings or root around in something that is not their business. If somebody asks and I say that she is dead they often get embarrassed and start apologizing. Then I get embarrassed too. Grief is not something you talk about.

I was only two weeks old when my mother, Eva, died. She only lived for a few days after the stroke that took her life. Nobody had understood that she was ill, so it was a terrible shock for everyone. I often wonder how Dad coped during that time, with me as a newborn baby and my sister who was then two years old.

I have been told how happy Eva was to become a mother for the second time. Before my sister arrived Dad and Mum had been quite worried that they would not be able to have children, so their happiness was enormous. It feels wonderful to know that I was a much longed-for child. It feels cruel and unjust that a new mother whose great longing for a family has at last been fulfilled should be torn away from her children. Even if we only had 14 days together I hope that she had time to hold me and rock me in her arms, to sniff my baby smell and love me.

After my mother died and left us, my father, Jonas, had to take upon himself the role of mother too. He fetched frozen breast milk from other mothers at the hospital and fed me with a bottle. Dad had to take all the responsibility on his own and he did it remarkably well. Things did not turn out as anyone thought they would. We were three people in our family not four, but that worked out alright too. We have had to take care of each other and I feel very close to Dad. We have the same sense of humour and often think the same. I love my sister above all else. She is my best friend.

My sister and I have had to manage without a mother in the background telling us how to behave. Instead of a gap between parents and children, as in other families, Dad, my sister and I became a little gang. She and I have always had a say in the decision-making. When we were small Dad almost always asked us what we thought, which clothes we wanted to wear and what we wanted for dinner. We had rules too, but they were never a big issue. I remember my childhood as being very happy.

Sometimes I wonder what it would have been like if Mum had died when I was older. Which of the two would have been worse? The grief would have been different. My grief is of another type than that of somebody who has only just lost a loved one. I never really had a chance to be her daughter. For me she is more of an idol and a role model. If she had died now, I would probably be sick with grief. But I would have had more of her with me in my life. Now I only have the mother I create for myself, but it feels as though I know her anyway. By listening to people and looking at pictures I have gained an idea of what she was like. In that way she is alive for me.

I have often heard my friends complaining about their tiresome mothers, perhaps mostly when we were a couple of years younger and our teenage rebellion was at its worst. Then I usually got angry. Didn't they realize that they were the luckiest kids in the world because they had their own proper mothers? Okay, a mother they argued with every day just then, who 'didn't understand a thing'. But anyway a mother to love and be loved by. A mother who could tell them what they were like when they were small and how they had kicked inside her tummy. A mother who comforted them, laughed, thought of things to do and who they could share their thoughts with. I would do anything to be able to change places with them.

I don't go around feeling sad and grieving every day, or even often. Mostly I'm very happy! But when things go badly for me and life feels rotten I get this feeling of loss. I realize then that Mum will never ever come back. That she has gone and that I will have to live my life without her.

At those times I hardly know how to carry on living with all that sorrow. It happens sometimes when a boy has left me, when I've had an argument with a friend or when everything feels grey and meaningless. Imagine if she had been there then. She would have been able to tell me about similar things that she had been through, shared her experiences with me and given me her love.

People who knew her say that she was one of the wisest and finest people in the world, and that she always cared about everyone around her, and therefore it feels so sad and unfair that I can't have her with me. It feels empty and lonely, like a hole inside me. Why did my mother of all people have to die? I never get specially picked out otherwise – never win a lottery or anything. It would have been Mum and me against the world! What would being dumped by a boyfriend matter if I had a mother to be comforted by?

But I'm like that too. It is true that one often doesn't see what one has got, only what one hasn't. What have I got in that case? An absolutely fantastic, considerate father, the main basis of my sense of security, my role model and really terrific. A big sister who loves me just as much. She has become the one who is caring and wise and a kind of substitute for a mother.

When I was three Dad met my stepmother who has been living with us since I was ten. My 'other mother' as I said when I was little. They have got two sons, my kid brothers who are now five and two years old. Not to mention my 'bonus granny' as she calls herself. She is one of the best people on earth!

Even though I have lost probably the one most important person in my life I have a lot of people around me who mean all the world to me. I have found it very easy to turn to adults around me. But it can be difficult to think sensibly. Sometimes I don't care about all the things that I should be thankful for. At times when I feel vulnerable I just want to have Mum back.

Since I'm not religious I have no idea about what happens to one after death. If I were convinced that I would be able to meet Mum on the 'other side', then it would probably feel easier. But she's alive in some way. In one photo in my room she's laughing, in another she's looking serious. I have her diaries and photo album from when she was young. These are her way to tell me her own story. She exists in people who remember her. Every time somebody tells me about her she comes alive for me and I can feel her. She exists in my sister who has the same big brown eyes and thick brown hair. And in me. Dad says that we have the same laugh and that makes me happy. I'm part of her. Half of my DNA-spiral comes from my mother. It feels nice to have an origin and inherited characteristics. I too have a mother. Instead of getting depressed I try to live in a way that would make her proud. Wherever she is – lying on a cloud amongst the angels or perhaps sitting in a bar in heaven discussing gender issues while having a beer with Anna Lindh? Wherever she is I want her to look after me and keep a watchful eye on all of us who miss her.

Sometimes I talk to Mum, although I think then that I'm a bit crazy. Not aloud, I converse with her in my head when I miss her more than usual. Then I can say or think that I would like her to be here, and want her to be as proud of me as I am of her.

I love Mum. Even as a dead person she is my mother and I hope we'll meet again. I try to persuade myself that we will, because the thought that we won't is too hard. It would be awful if she really was gone for ever and didn't exist in any shape or form, as a spirit or part of some greater being. If there was just emptiness, air. No, it simply can't be that way.

I comfort myself that when I have children I'm going to try to be the mother I never had, do everything to be a good and understanding parent. I hope and believe that I've been shaped by the woman I've heard such fine stories about. I probably have a little of her sense of humour, involvement, love, thoughts and strength. I know what she was enthusiastic about, what she did for others and how much happiness she spread, and I'm spurred on by that. For a start I'm in Paris reading French at the Sorbonne.

A couple of years ago there was a programme on TV about the women's movement in the 1970s. For the first time I got to see Mum on film, singing with her group Red Beans. There she stood, full of life, singing and moving about! It was fantastic. I really felt then that she exists. I try to picture her like that when I miss her most.

It is not a matter of course to have two parents alive. Even if both one's parents are alive, it is no guarantee that they will both be a part of one's life. Lots of people have little or no contact with one or other parent, usually the father, and that must also be very sad. While I can feel sorry for other people who have lost one of their loved ones, it can at the same time be comforting for me that I am not alone. The thoughts that I think, others think too. Through having tasted grief I have greater understanding for others. One grows through one's experiences, gets stronger and understands better what is valuable in life.

I have learnt that it is not dangerous to be sad. Sorrow like joy is a part of life. My aunt, who is one of my 'extra mothers', says that it is just as natural to cry as to laugh. She is right. I do not believe that one can live a whole life without falling into one or another grief-hole in the road. But I believe that one can always pick oneself up again. For me grief has never been charged with anxiety or panic since my mother has 'always been dead'. But I have grieved nevertheless.

Kristoffer and Alexander

'This whole year has been bad and good.
I haven't been in tears for ages. … I've forgotten the
number of his mobile. I want it.'

Kristoffer was born in 1994 and Alexander in 1996.
They were eight and six years old, respectively, when they lost their father,
Lukas.

Lukas my dad. I feel very sad, because he was my dad. Lukas was away when he died. He died an awful death in a parachute accident. Right after Lukas had died I got nightmares because I was sad and under pressure. I imagined that parts of Lukas's body were lying spread all over the valley. The nightmares stopped when me and Mum and my little brother had been to see Dad in the mortuary. I didn't go up to him because I was afraid. I stood by the wall, but I saw him. He was whole. Then angels came into my dreams and the nightmares disappeared. Lukas said once that he flew with angels in a basejump. He died in Engelsberg.

I would like to have my dad back because we were a family and we had fun together.

For a long time my great interest was the underground. On Saturdays Dad and I went on the underground. Our aim was to see every single station. We bought soft drinks, sweets and crisps to take with us and sometimes we got off at a station that I wanted to have an extra look at. My brother was allowed to come with us in his stroller, but he usually didn't find it such fun.

This whole year has been bad and good. It's good that I'm not sad all the time. When I am sad I talk to Mum. And I haven't been in tears for ages.

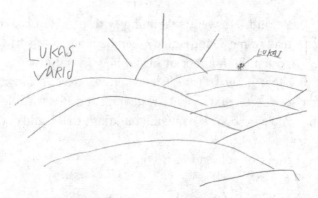

'Lukas's world' drawn by Kristoffer as he received the news of the death.

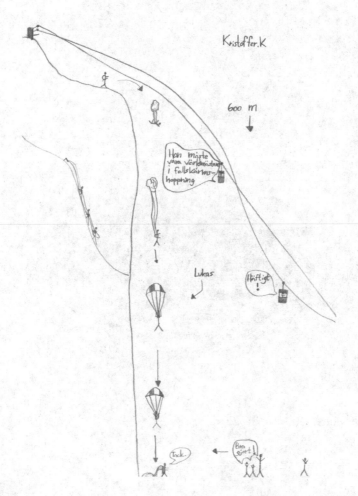

'World champion' by Kristoffer. 'He must be the world champion in parachute jumping.' 'Great!'
'Well done!' 'Thanks.'

My daddy was kind. He went swimming with me. He played football with me and read to me. Daddy died when he jumped. It's bad that he's dead. I've forgotten the number of his mobile. I want it.

It's a pity that he wasn't with us when we were in Singapore. He should have seen us when we sat in a restaurant and ate sushi and the food arrived on a conveyor belt. We saw tall buildings that Daddy could have jumped from.

Daddy, I think of you and miss you.

LUKAS SON ALEXANDER

Alexander calls his drawing 'Crashed bodies'.

Julia

*'If your mother dies when you're
little, then you are used to it by
the time you are a grown-up.'*

Julia was born in 1991.
She was five years old when she lost her mother, Christina.
(Julia's little sister, Norah, tells her story on page 159.)

It was the first day of domestic science in Grade 8. We had a new teacher and we were supposed to be getting to know her. She asked each of us questions and when she got to me she asked: 'And what does your mother do?' Total silence filled the room. Everyone stared at me. Words failed me for a few seconds. It hurt to say: 'She isn't alive any more.'

The night it happened I woke up. Something was wrong. Dad was worried but I went back to bed again, because I was tired.

In the morning I got up as usual and went into the kitchen. A woman I didn't know was standing there doing the washing-up. 'Where's Mummy?' I asked (in English, because we lived in Mummy's country, Australia, at that time). She looked at me with no expression on her face. Then I can't remember how I found out that Mummy was dead, because I was only five years old.

One day we arrived at a large building where everything was white. We went into the building and suddenly she was lying there. She had on a white dress. There was total silence. Mummy wasn't breathing. Her face was pale and quite cold. Nothing happened when I touched her.

I remember that Dad and my little sister Norah, who was three, sat beside her looking at her sadly. That was the last time I ever saw my mother.

She was given a nice place for her grave, near a forest. Every time we are in Australia we go and visit her and put flowers on her grave.

We and Dad moved back to Sweden and everybody here in this whole neighbourhood talked about what had happened. Mummy, Christina, was known for spreading light and happiness round about her. It feels as though she is always here among us anyway. I know that she is somewhere watching over us. I can feel it.

And I believe in ghosts. I know because I have seen one. In the evening when I was just about to fall asleep I saw a blue light in the dark room. The blue light got bigger and bigger and I saw somebody. Then I saw who it was. It was the person I've had in my heart ever since the day I first saw her: Mummy! I was scared at first, but I soon calmed down, because she said something to me that I will always keep to myself. Then she disappeared and I felt peaceful and relaxed. It was like in a dream.

One day at playschool in Australia I had done a painting of Mummy. I had painted her long dark hair and happy face. She was so happy when I gave it to her: 'Ooooohhh Julia! Have you painted this?' She covered it in plastic film and always had it on the wall. I still have that painting and I will always keep it. I also have all her books in which she's underlined things. Dad gives us 50 kronor for every book we read, but that isn't necessary with Mummy's books.

There is no way to explain how much I miss her.

We've made a little memorial garden here in the forest down by the lake and we've planted a tiny fir tree that is Mummy's. We often go to 'Mummy's garden' and light candles, on her birthday, on Mother's Day or just when we feel like it. I think it's a good thing, because then we can go and talk to her. She is always there.

I think that a lot would have been different if Mummy had lived. Perhaps we would still have been living in Australia. I love my home country, Australia, where I was born. I think I'll go and live there when I grow up, and I would like to have Mummy's surname.

Mummy dying is good, almost, in one way: I can comfort others with the same problem, because I know what it feels like. It would probably be harder to lose Mummy now. When you are little you have time to learn to look after yourself. Otherwise I would have got used to having Mummy there all the time. If your mother dies when you're little, then you are used to it by the time you are a grown-up.

I know that I will meet Mummy again sometime, somewhere, I just know it!

Sten

'He had left a note in the kitchen.
It said that he had gone down
to the sea for a while.'

Sten was born in 1989.
When he was nine years old he lost his father, Örjan.
(Sten's older sister, Tove, tells her story on page 131.)

Dad died in 1999. He took his own life. That he could do so was and still is one of the biggest mysteries for me. Unfortunately it is likely to remain just that, a mystery.

Dad

My father was born in 1955. This means that when I was born in September 1989 he was 34 and working as a teacher of history, geography and Swedish. He devoted most of his leisure time to his family, the garden and literature. At one time he ran a book café. He had an interest that was so great that it could be called a passion. It was to translate the poems of a Uruguayan poet. They met when our family (I had not been born yet) spent three months in Uruguay and Dad worked as a freelance journalist. He spoke good Spanish thanks to the fact that he had travelled around in Bolivia as a 17-year-old.

I first learnt about Dad's great social involvement after his death. He was a member of the Left Party and wrote a number of political articles. He travelled a lot in a way that is uncommon nowadays. He knew a lot about the inhabitants and made contact with people of the country that he was in. That meant that he got to see a lot of poverty and for him the sight of a poor child was like the stab of a knife in his tremendously kind heart.

Dad often felt very bad and suffered from depression. I didn't notice that he was depressed at the time. He made a lot of effort to keep it from my sister, Tove, and me. In 1998 Dad was so unhappy that he felt that he needed a change in his life. He applied to a college of journalism and was one of 20 to be accepted out of 200 applicants. The course was one year long. That year he stayed at his best friend's house in another town and he came home at weekends. I don't remember having any problem with Dad not being at home during the week.

Now, afterwards, I have a very divided view of the time Dad spent away. On the one hand I can be thankful and see it as a way of getting used to being without him. On the other hand I would have liked to have spent more time with him during the last year of his life.

When I have listened to relatives and friends who knew Dad as a child and who knew how he was feeling as an adult, a number of things have turned up that might have contributed. One of the many things was that he had twice been separated from his parents for a time when he was a small child.

From the age of one he had to live at his aunt's because Grandma and Grandpa couldn't look after him just then. Grandma was living at a kind of nurses' training college while on her nursing course and for Grandpa it was not a particularly drastic decision to leave the little boy with his sister-in-law. At that time it was quite common for close relatives to take care of each other's children.

After the whole family had moved around the country and even spent some months in France, they were sent to Brazzaville in the Congo. Grandma and Grandpa were missionaries and Dad had to live at a boarding school with other missionaries' children. He started there when he was eight and he had turned 11 and spent three years of his childhood at the school by the time they moved back to Sweden. The only exceptions were the Easter, Christmas and summer holidays that he was allowed to spend with his parents. Apart from the holidays, letters were the only form of communication he had with his parents.

Dad's life deep down inside was marked by a strong feeling of longing for his mother, caused by these two 'separations'.

Death

This fateful day is one that I both remember and do not remember. Up until the moment I learnt about his death I remember most things quite clearly, but afterwards what I remember is mostly what I have been told.

The 24 April 1999 was a Saturday. The evening before, I had been at a youth club and played ping-pong with a friend. Looking back, I have often been struck by guilt because I wasn't at home with Dad that last day. In the evening Dad had wanted to lie in bed beside me till I went to sleep. First I tried to put him off, saying that it was not necessary, but in the end what happened was that he lay and held me in his arms until I fell asleep.

When we woke up he had left a note in the kitchen. It said that he had gone down to the sea for a while.

One memory that is very vivid for me is the last time I thought that every-thing was as usual. It was in the bathroom when I asked Tove where Dad was and she told me what it said in the note, that he was down by the sea. I didn't find that at all strange then.

The morning passed slowly and we began to get a bit worried. It is in the midst of this anxiety that started gnawing inside us that my memory becomes more and more vague. When a policeman rang later on and informed us that they had found a car somewhere, registered in Mum's name, my anxiety turned into an inferno.

The policeman requested a description and Mum said that if they were going to search for him, we would come straight over. The police-man said that it would be better if we stayed at home. While we were waiting for new information from the police I remember that we started speculating wildly, and that it was Tove who first mentioned the risk that he had taken his own life. We tried to convince each other that it was probably nothing special, but inside me the fear that he had taken his life had started to grow.

We watched *101 Dalmatians* to try and get away from the anxiety if possible. It is now completely impossible for me to see that film. I also remember that I went upstairs and watched an ice-hockey match between Sweden and the Czech Republic. I was sitting there trying to watch hockey when Mum called me. I asked what she wanted and said that I was watching hockey. She told me once again to come downstairs and when she said she had something to tell us I did as I was told. I was instantly sure that this terrible thing had happened, that Dad was dead. My inner self was convinced then, but my outer self refused to take it in and tried to push away those thoughts.

When Mum, Tove and I eventually sat down on the sofa, Granny and Grandad and a couple of good friends had arrived. I don't remember the exact words but this is approximately what Mum said: 'Now I'm going to tell you the hardest thing I've ever had to tell you: Daddy is dead. He chose it himself.'

My inner self exploded. I cried until there were no more tears.

I don't know how long we sat there on the sofa and held each other, Mum, Tove and I, but I remember that between sobs we gulped out things like 'Why our dad?' and 'It's not fair!'

What I remember about the rest of the day is that our friends and Granny and Grandad stayed with us. We didn't manage to eat much and I think we went for a walk.

The days after

The days that followed were the darkest in my life. The grief was enormous but I only cried inside myself. People we knew arrived with flowers, said how sad they were and had coffee that somebody had brewed.

Dad's father, brother and one of his uncles came to our home the very first night. In the middle of everything I remember a conflict that arose about who should be the first to see Dad when he was dead. I do not remember the exact details, just that somebody who was going to travel back home wanted to see the body. But Tove and I wanted absolutely to be the first to see the body. Looking back, one can see this as petty of Tove and me, but just then it meant a great deal to us that they didn't overlook us just because we were children. Thanks to Mum it turned out as Tove and I wanted.

I remember the fear of seeing Dad as a corpse. What we were really afraid of is hard to say now, but I imagine that what scared us was that then there would be no doubt that he was dead. That is what it meant to see him in the mortuary.

Despite the fear, we went into the chilly room where he was lying. To see Dad when he was dead was almost as much a good thing as it was sad. He lay on a stretcher in his ordinary clothes and it felt right that he did not have on some white gown, because that would have made him seem more unfamiliar.

Tove and I were each allowed to close one of Dad's eyes and I remember that his cold skin felt rather unpleasant at first. We had time to start getting used to it though, since we held him and kissed his dead hands for most of the time. I am glad that we saw him when he was dead, because I can imagine that I would otherwise have begun imagining things that would have been as idiotic as they were tragic, that it was in fact not my father who had died.

I have no idea how long we spent in the room. As was often the case during those black days my sense of time was non-existent. It was in there that I said a final farewell to my father.

Some weeks later Mum and I quarrelled about whether or not I should be allowed to see the pictures that Dad had painted during his therapy. That I was not allowed to see them felt to me like a betrayal and I can still remember how powerless I felt against all the grown-ups.

On Wednesday the week after Dad died I started school again. On the Monday I had already received a little book of drawings and every pupil had also written a short comforting message. It felt good to know that everyone knew what had happened before I arrived at school.

One thing I remember is that our teacher changed the seating order in the classroom so that I could sit next to my best friend.

I also remember that it was upsetting to talk about Dad with my friends. I understand now that getting back to school so quickly was a way of trying to escape into ordinary daily life. A way for me to survive when I felt that I couldn't cope with bearing the enormous grief and emptiness.

The funeral

On the Friday two weeks after Dad's death he was to have his funeral in the church where Tove, Mum and I had been christened and where Mum and Dad had been married. On the day of the funeral Tove, Mum and I had decorated Dad's coffin with the help of a florist. It took quite a long time and I remember that I thought it was rather tiring. Flower arrangement has never been my strong point.

We saw Dad for the last time on the day of the funeral and it was just as beautiful then.

When the funeral service was due to start the church was jam-packed. I remember that in the middle of all the crying I felt quite proud that so many people had come to grieve over Dad and to show their sympathy. When we went into the church I cried, cried as I had not done since the time I was told of Dad's death.

The funeral was wonderful, with lovely singing and an enormous procession of mourners filing past the coffin. When they had passed by the coffin and kissed it or left flowers or incense sticks (one of Dad's friends was a Buddhist and at Buddhist funerals incense sticks are a tradition) they walked past us and nodded sympathetically on their way back to their places.

Just about everybody turned to Mum with their sympathetic nods. I remember how much I appreciated it when somebody turned to Tove and me instead. When the ceremony was over we walked in a procession to the site that had been chosen for the grave. Mum, Tove and I walked behind the six coffin bearers who led the way out of the church.

When the burial was over it was time for sandwiches. All the speeches that I would certainly appreciate now just bored me and we children went outside to play instead. I would really like to have them written down so that I could read them now.

I carry the funeral with me in my life as a very beautiful memory.

Dad and me

I have always been very close to both my parents. When Dad was alive I was just a little child and had the relationship with Dad that one has with one's father when one is a child.

Dad was never a great sports enthusiast and it sometimes disappointed me that neither of my parents had a genuine interest in football.

Since I've grown older I've noticed with some sadness how many interests Dad and I would have had in common if only he had not chosen to escape from life. Peace and aid issues lie within both Dad's and my fields of interest. The fact that Dad was fluent in Spanish would have been a great joy to me since I too am reading Spanish now.

My relationship with Dad was just as good as it could have been. He was enormously popular among my friends, because he was a master at telling stories and organizing games. He gave me all this and a lot more, and for this I feel grateful to him.

I am convinced that he was in fact absolutely the best possible father for me. But all the things that we missed out on since we never had the opportunity of knowing each other for more than nine years make me feel infinitely sad. I will have to live with that sadness for the rest of my life.

In my situation one can choose to be bitter or thankful. One can't choose to avoid one or the other completely, but one can emphasize thankfulness or bitterness. I hope and believe that I have chosen to put the emphasis on thankfulness. I am thankful for having been allowed to get to know the father I love, who gave me so much of his love and so many of his values.

How life is now

My life after Dad's death has been very good. We stayed on the farm until I had finished Grade 6. Then we moved to a big city where I now live, go to school and play football.

When Mum met a new husband it affected me rather negatively at first and I saw it as a betrayal of Dad, but began to accept it later on. I understand now that Dad would not have wanted Mum to go through life alone and only devote herself to grieving over him. We live together with Mum's new husband and his two children and are almost like a family. I have not chosen anyone as my 'new father' and that feels incredibly far away. I would never be able to find a substitute for Dad even if I have got a fair number of adult male role models. Not a day passes without my thinking about Dad, although now it is no longer the sad thoughts that are uppermost in my mind.

I don't find it as upsetting nowadays when somebody asks about Dad. On the contrary, I sometimes even find that it feels right when close friends get to know who he was and what his death has meant to me. But sometimes I still get landed in situations when it feels hard to talk about it.

And I sometimes have a bad conscience because I don't think about Dad enough. I think that is stupid, but I can't do anything about it.

A lot has changed because of Dad's death, but there are also things that have not changed. My love for him will not change for as long as I live.

Ebba

*'We all went up to Mummy and sat
with her until she had slipped away.'*

Ebba was born in 1991.
She was ten years old when she lost her mother, Marianne.

My beloved mother Marianne, Mallan as she was known, had a close friend with whom she took long walks every evening, and I went with them when I felt like it.

She said that she thought that one of Mummy's breasts looked a bit bigger than the other. 'Huh, it's because I breastfed with that breast,' said Mummy. But she went and had her breasts checked, to see that it was not anything dangerous.

One day when I came home from school and went out into the kitchen I saw Mummy talking on the phone. I noticed that it was a rather serious conversation. When she had put down the receiver she sat down on a chair and cried. I sat on her lap and tried to comfort her and asked what had happened. 'The lady who rang was from the hospital and she said that I've got breast cancer.' I hugged Mummy harder and harder with all the strength in my heart. I cried and cried, I knew that it was a dangerous illness, but my mother was the strongest in the world. She would cope with this. Mummy said that there was no danger, she would totally regain her health, it would just take time.

Time passed. We didn't think very often about the fact that Mummy was ill, but sometimes it struck me that she really did have breast cancer. She was still the same wonderful, happy mother and my life carried on as usual. I knew that of course Mummy would regain her health. I loved my family and my friends and felt that I really did have their support.

The winter passed and summer arrived. As soon as school ended we went out to our summer cottage, just as lovely as always. I spent all day every day with my friends and I think we lay in the water at least half of the time. It was a glorious summer, but all good things come to an end.

The autumn arrived and Mummy got worse. She was on chemotherapy and radiation treatment. She was the strongest mother in the world. I loved her most of all and was given so much love by her.

Mummy rang Granny every day and talked and talked. She took long walks with Granny, with Grandma (Dad's mother), or with one of her millions of friends, who were all quite fantastic.

The winter passed and turned to spring. Mummy loved the spring. As early as February she used to sit in her bra on the terrace and sunbathe. Mummy and I used to go out cycling and have competitions about who would be the first to hear the nightingale, and of course it was Mummy.

She had been given so much chemotherapy and had so much radiation treatment that she lost her hair. But she had a very nice wig and wasn't at all embarrassed to be seen without it. Mummy told everybody that she had breast cancer and she wasn't afraid to say it.

It was summer again. We had a wonderful time as usual. The garden beds were flowering, it was boiling hot and I lay in the water and splashed around. Mummy and I competed at being the first to swim out to the buoy. Sometimes I got there before her, but Mummy was really fast. When she was first she sat on it and teased me, but it was just for fun.

The autumn came and turned grey, the winter came, and spring came again. In the meantime the cancer spread to almost her whole body: her bones, liver and lungs. Mummy got sicker day by day, but it was nothing that I thought about.

My older sister's boyfriend was going to have his graduation party and Mummy and Dad were invited. Mummy was going to buy clothes for the party, but typically for Mummy she couldn't decide whether to have the pink or the gold trousers, so she bought both pairs. Mummy and I often spent time in town shopping for clothes.

At the party Mummy was happy as usual, dancing and having fun. But only a few days later when all of us children in the neighbourhood were out playing, Dad came and fetched me. I didn't know why he had come because they usually let me go home on my own.

Dad held my hand and said that Mummy had got pneumonia and was in hospital. I felt scared, because I didn't know whether pneumonia was a dangerous illness.

After a few days she came home, but now things went from bad to worse extremely fast. She went into hospital more and more often. Got more and more tired. In the end she couldn't even walk upstairs to her bedroom, and Dad had to help her. But it got even worse.

My heart grew heavier and heavier, but I knew that Mummy was strong. She would make it. But I think that Dad knew that time was soon up for Mummy. Dad was just as strong. He was able to keep his anger to himself and he never showed his sadness. There were many evenings when I cried and Dad always came and comforted me.

One weekend I was going to stay with one of my best friends. She and I always thought of things to do and it was always fun to be at her place. Her mother fetched me. I forgot to say goodbye to Mummy.

On Saturday we visited the zoo and I bought a present for Mummy since it was Mother's Day the next day: a dream-catcher to have in her bedroom so that she wouldn't have nightmares. After lunch my friend's mother received a telephone call. She talked for quite a long time and then I was allowed to talk. I moved a little way away from the others. It was Dad. He said that Mummy had taken a turn for the worse and that I should come home. I really did not want to. I wanted to go home to my friend's and mess about. But in the end I went home.

Everyone was at home when I arrived, even Granny. She was clearly going to spend the night at our house. After dinner I had been invited to a party in our neighbourhood. I should of course have been at my friend's but now I went to the party instead.

When I had come back home from the party, brushed my teeth and got into bed, Dad came and said goodnight. We talked for a long, long time. He said that Mummy didn't have much time left. And that I wasn't to go into Mummy's room because she was so troubled. I think that it was the first time that Dad cried with me, but we cried quietly, so as not to upset Mummy. We cried and cried and talked about everything.

Dad hugged me and I slept well and deeply. In the morning they were going to let me give Mummy her present.

It was morning and the most beautiful day of the year. The flowers were flowering, the birds were singing and the sun was shining. I went down and had breakfast and asked Dad if I could give Mummy her present.

I went in cautiously and saw that Mummy was glad to see me. Dad stood in the doorway waiting. As soon as I got into the room it was as though a wave of grief crashed over me. I couldn't keep my tears back. I turned and wanted to run away. I couldn't cope. But with Dad standing there I felt support and dared to go up to Mummy.

I crouched down beside her. We gazed at each other for a while. Then I opened her present for her.

I think it made her happy. I could tell that she wasn't going to make it. I would have done anything at all to see Mummy healthy again, but I knew it was impossible. I talked to Mummy for a while. As soon as I got out of the room I burst into tears.

In the porch I saw Grandma, with a basket filled with food as usual. She sat down on the sofa with my younger sisters and held them close to her as though she wanted to protect them from something. I sat down in the armchair opposite them. She told them that Mummy didn't have long to live. They started to cry. Grandma hugged them and looked at me. I saw tears deep inside her eyes.

We all went up to Mummy and sat there, close to her, until she had slipped away.

What I remember most was my older brother. That hurt me the most. I had never seen him cry before. It was as if someone stabbed a knife into his heart. It hurt so much to see him.

We were allowed to sit with Mummy as much as we wanted. I sat with her for over two hours. I cried and talked to her, but it was not at all as it used to be. Because Mummy was dead. I lay close to her. She was cold, but that's what it's like when someone dies. I wanted to warm her.

During the day flowers arrived for us that filled the whole house. From all our friends. I got a wonderful bouquet from my best friend and it warmed my heart.

At four o'clock in the afternoon the hearse came and fetched Mummy. I vented my anger and grief on the people who took Mummy away from me. I will never ever see my mummy again.

I had cried so much and just wanted to go and lie down and die as well. I slept in the same bed as my younger sister, because I didn't want to sleep alone that night.

The day after, none of us went to school. Dad, my older brother, my older sister and I went to a funeral parlour. There we chose the urn and the coffin. The bloody old bag sitting there was cold and unfeeling. She just wanted to get a move on and get it over and done with.

In the afternoon a friend looked in with a card that my classmates had made. On it they had written such beautiful things that I started to cry. It was quite upsetting that everyone knew about it, because some of them came up to me at break with masses of unpleasant questions that hurt. Although sooner or later they would have found out about it anyway.

Our vicar arrived after a couple of days, the one we were to have for the funeral. He was my older sister's friend's father, so we knew him quite well. We talked about what he was going to say about us and Mummy. Then we had to choose the music. Mummy's favourite songs were one by Ulf Lundell and one by Evert Taube. When we chose Ulf Lundell's song the vicar expressed his opinion that it was not much good in church, because alcohol is mentioned in the lyrics. But we really wanted it and in the end we got what we wanted.

Just before the funeral I was out in the garden and picked masses of flowers. Mummy loved our garden. I wanted her to have the most beautiful flowers.

We took a taxi to the church. I had never seen what it looked like before I went in. The music started to play and we had to walk slowly through the sorrowful church to get to the places where we were to sit. As soon as I got inside the doors I burst into tears, against my will. I saw Mummy's coffin up there at the front with all the beautiful flowers around it. It felt as though the whole world was watching me while I was crying.

The church was filled with Mummy's friends. We had chosen a big church so that there would be room for everybody. The vicar spoke about how beautiful Mummy was and all the wonderful times we had had with her. When they played and sang the Ulf Lundell song I couldn't control myself. Tears gushed out of my eyes. I wanted to run away and scream. It was so beautiful and I missed Mummy so much that I wanted to die.

When my older brother saw me crying he comforted me and put his arms around me. I will never forget that as long as I live. Then we went forward one by one and put a flower on the coffin.

Afterwards everyone gathered in a building where we ate and talked.

The summer came and went and I was at a sailing camp with friends and had a lot of fun. But when evening came I just wanted to go back home. Not a single evening passed without my crying or longing for Dad and Mummy and the family. Other years I have almost never rung home, never felt homesick. Now that Mummy was dead I felt anxious all the time. Just imagine if something happened to Dad. I was frightened and wanted to know that everyone was alright.

Dad had to comfort me on a lot of evenings, but it felt very embarrassing to say 'I long for Mummy'.

The autumn came. We had a headstone for Mummy and it was time for the burial. It was upsetting to stand there and see the urn with Mummy's body in it sink down into the earth.

I have had a lot of good times, but also a lot of difficult ones. Now I see it like this: you only live once and you must make the most out of life.

Sometimes I feel different. My friends and I can find totally different things important. I am more serious and understand more, since I have lost my mother. I know how it feels and what it's like. They can never put themselves in my position. However much they say 'I understand'.

When Mummy had just died I believed I would never be able to go on living without her. It is a strength and a prop for me that I really can live without Mummy – although it is hard. I love Mummy and I will love her for ever until the last day of my life.

Armin

'It's easier for me when people don't talk about Mummy than when they do.'

Armin was born in 1991.
He was five years old when he lost his mother, Ferida.

My parents, my sister and I came to Sweden at the beginning of 1993. Mummy and Dad started quarrelling in 1995 because Dad went boozing with his friends too much. After they had been quarrelling for a year they separated.

Dad arrived early in the morning one day and broke into an empty flat next to ours. When he had broken in he waited in that flat for Mummy and that time he was drunk. When he saw Mummy leave for work he dragged her into the flat and strangled her.

Then I don't know what happened, but I do know that he went to the police station and reported that he had killed his wife, that is, my mother.

A policeman we knew visited us just before I was due to leave for day care and he told us that our mother had died. When I heard this I ran into my room and covered my head with a pillow and just cried. My sister came in and comforted me and when I had calmed down she rang and told my day care teacher everything that had happened and they let me stay at home for a couple of weeks.

My sister rang Mummy's best friend and told her what had happened too. Mummy's friend came to our home straightaway and comforted us. She stayed with us overnight and slept here and so did her daughter who is two years older than me. She and I used to play together a lot at that time as well.

Since then I have felt grief inside me. For every year that passes I think that I'm starting to forget it, but I don't. I just feel that way.

It's easier for me when people don't talk about Mummy than when they do. When somebody mentions Mummy I remember things we did together. But I have a grandma, a grandpa and a sister who look after me. Grandma and Grandpa moved to our home in Sweden after Mummy died. Now they are like a mother and a father to me, the only difference is that they are older.

Dad had to stay in prison for six years and then he was deported from Sweden for ever in 2001, in November. We have been in touch with him all the time and still are. We ring each other once a week and send text messages every day. Grandma, Grandpa, my sister and I go and visit him every Christmas and summer holiday.

When I was younger everybody used to tease me when I caused trouble, but I just used to tease back. Now everyone has understood that I don't have a mother and they don't tease me any more. I have learnt not to tease people who have a mother, or people who don't have a mother. When Mummy died I mostly wanted help during the early days. Nowadays I have the help that I've got used to.

Dad and I almost never talk about Mummy. I tried once, but then Dad just wanted to talk about something else. I understood, because I'm sure it's not something that he wants to remember. He just wants to forget it all instead, I think.

I think that I can forgive Dad for what he has done. When he did it I was only little. He has done good things for me, but a very bad thing anyway by killing Mummy. Dad has changed and only drinks soft drinks with his friends.

I don't feel as sad now as I did before and I think about the fact that Grandma has taken Mummy's place in my life and that it has worked out very well so far.

If I ever feel sad I go into a room with my sister and we talk about things, but that was more when I was younger. I don't talk about it so much nowadays, but if somebody teases me about Mummy for example, and I get very sad, I talk to my sister and she comforts me.

At school there is a welfare officer who is kind. She says that I can come and talk to her if I want to. I don't want to. But it is good that she says it.

I used to go out and play with my friends before. Now I mostly sit around and think about if you can be born again and live a new life. I hope so, because then Mummy can live again and I can visit her.

Sometimes I go out with my friend. I find that I can talk freely then about whatever I want to, and that's what I do with my friend. Once my friend and I talked about what happens when you die. We thought that you could live a new life again after death. If you had been good, then you would be born normal without any illnesses. I hope that I can live again and if I can then I will search for Mummy and find her and talk to her.

A lovely memory of Mummy is on my fifth birthday. A lot of my friends were invited and Mummy said that I must switch on the radio/cassette player as I had learnt to do and I put on a cassette with Dad's songs. When I had turned on the music everyone started dancing. It was great fun because everyone danced in any way they felt like. I will remember that for the rest of my life. I hope so.

Mummy lived till she was 38. Her name was Ferida and I think that is a very nice name.

Even if I would like to turn the clock back and even though grief is always there in my heart, I try to live a happy life. I go to school and enjoy my childhood in my own way. In my spare time I do boxing.

I don't enjoy myself as much in the wintertime because then I spend most of my time indoors, but in the summer I do, when I run around with my friends and have fun. When I grow up I am going to be a policeman. I am 13 years old now.

Armin

Madeleine

'A few years passed before I started
to miss having a mother.'

Madeleine was born in 1985.
When she was three years old she lost her mother, Ewa.

One day when I was just over six months old Mummy was running to catch the bus when she collapsed. Her legs did not want to carry her. After many long hours of waiting and painful tests at the hospital, she was told that she had fallen ill with myeloma. It is a type of cancer of the bone marrow that slowly changes the bone structure and causes intense pain in the bones and breaks down the whole body until one has no strength even to breathe. And worst of all: there was no cure. Mummy was not going to live for very much longer.

In the beginning, during my first year, she was at home quite a lot. She tried to take care of me and my four-year-old brother and to show her love as well as she could, but as time passed Dad and Grandma had to take over more and more.

There were many trips to the hospital to start different treatments. I remember one time in particular. I asked Dad when Mummy was going to come home, and he replied 'at the weekend'. So I hung around at home waiting and when Friday arrived at last the ambulance turned up with Mummy. But she was very tired and had no energy to talk. She was put straight to bed and my brother and I were told not to disturb her. Almost immediately the ambulance turned up again, this time to fetch her. The pain was too intense and it needed to be soothed by painkillers.

Her indescribable pain could not be relieved by thoughtfulness and closeness alone. It demanded a pain control so strong that it had to be given at a hospice or a hospital. That was no help to me. I felt forsaken and tears ran down my uncomprehending face when the ambulance left with Mummy.

Another time when Mummy was actually at home we had a masseur who came to soften up her muscles. I remember that when I sat there on the edge of the bed and watched her being massaged I was quite sure that she was not in pain just at that moment. It may only be a child's naive way of seeing things but since I was also allowed to help knead her body I felt that I could help her too. I was allowed to take part and still remember the red vibrating apparatus that you could pull along the length of your back so that it tickled all the way down to your toes.

That autumn when I was three and a half years old, Mummy passed away in hospital, and I can't remember crying. The whole world seemed to be in tears except me and I did not understand why. That day we were fetched earlier than usual, by a woman who was a family acquaintance, but I do not think that we went to the hospital to say goodbye. My brother was about to turn seven and was supposed to be starting school a week later, in the first grade. He tried to keep up his courage.

The funeral was exactly like the day she died. I felt uneasy but most of all uncomprehending. Wasn't there anybody who could tell me why everybody was so sad, and what it was that had happened? There were just a lot of people standing round a hole in the ground and staring at a box. I held on tightly to Dad's hand and looked up at him and asked: 'Why are you crying, Daddy?' Tears started to pour out of the eyes that I was looking into as he answered: 'I don't know.'

A few years passed before I started to miss having a mother. I was in the third grade and perhaps girls of that age are very much mothers' girls. There was a lot of 'Me and Mummy are going shopping for clothes today,' or 'Mummy and I,' and I understood early on that Dad just wasn't like the other girls' mothers.

Dad used to rush into a shop and I was given ten minutes to point out the clothes that I needed, while my friend's mother carefully chose matching garments for her daughter to wear. It was above all noticeable at school, as I used to have to wear my brother's outgrown sweaters, and I was probably what you would call a tomboy. Not that that bothered me, but it took quite a while before I began to feel 'girlish'.

We still lived in the house we had always lived in, and Dad probably had quite a hard time running his own business and looking after a home while at the same time caring for and bringing up two children.

Perhaps that was one of the reasons that there were always rather a lot of women in his life. They have therefore even been a part of mine, which has not always made me happy exactly. When I was little I turned to Dad's girlfriends and got attached to them as you do to a mother. But as they disappeared one by one so did my trust. I was often accused of having strong ties to Dad, a thing that they sometimes could not cope with and were jealous of.

Women came and went. As a little child I accepted them with much greater ease than when I became a teenager. I remember especially one of my dad's old girlfriends who wrote a letter where she spelled out in black and white that it was my fault that their relationship ended. She left the letter on my bed the day she moved out, and the time after that was dark for me. Dad became unemployed and depressed about this time. I felt my guilt deeply and it all led to my developing a weight problem.

But there were also a lot of brighter moments. Actually, I had and still have a very good relationship with my dad. I was given a lot of freedom and encouragement, whether it was a case of my wanting to play basketball or do karate. We have always lived in a large house with a lot of space, a pool and access to all sorts of equipment. I was given a dog when I turned 12, but it adopted Dad quite quickly, because it liked him more. You could say that we were well off and that I was a little bit spoilt.

Despite all these things I was a lonely child and did not attract any friends until I started school. Along with the friends, the friends' families entered my life, and most of all their mothers. From primary school until high school I went around a lot with a girl who was a year older than me. She and I were like sisters and I got two younger sisters into the bargain, and a mother. It suited me perfectly to be treated like a member of the family in their house, because then I got what I wanted most of all: a complete family.

Our families started seeing each other and we went on skiing holidays and travelled to Europe together. That mother is probably the woman who has influenced my development the most. I looked up to her and could confide anything at all to her. Unfortunately differences of opinion arose between our families and in the end I lost contact with my friend and her family.

The families of a lot of friends have the tendency to want to 'adopt' me as an extra daughter. During high school a classmate and I were as thick as thieves. We went on holiday with each other's families and slept over at each other's homes. The few times we were not to be seen together were only when one or other of us was really ill, so Dad called my friend Sticking Plaster.

Her mother has also played a great part in my life as a role model and mother-substitute. To me she was a cool mum and also a shoulder I could cry on when things were difficult. She was important when I didn't feel like talking to Dad about my teenage problems with boys and conflicts with friends.

The worst aspect of not having my own real mother will probably be when I myself am going to have a baby one day. Who am I going to talk to then? And who is my child going to call Granny?

Mummy was Polish so half of my roots are in Poland. Unfortunately I have lost contact with my Polish relatives. It feels sadder and sadder the older I get that I do not keep know the language alive by speaking it or anything about the culture in Mummy's home country.

I asked to read Polish as my home language at school, but they did not let me, since we did not keep that language alive by speaking it at home. Granny in Poland died last Christmas and I think I was nine when I was there last to visit them. She used to write to me. As a small child I could understand and speak a little Polish, but I forgot it as time passed. I still have a few relatives there and my brother and I have talked about going to visit them anyhow.

I am convinced that I would have had a stricter upbringing if Mummy had lived. But I would also have known her language – she was an interpreter – and known more about the country she grew up in.

The fact that Mummy passed away when I was so young has clearly changed a lot of things. It has probably made me stronger and more self-reliant, as I know that I am. Dad is mentally strong and he has certainly transferred some of that to me. He has always wanted the best for me and my brother and wants us to be able to look after ourselves. It is hard for me to see any real disadvantages. This is the way I have grown up – I don't know anything else and I feel optimistic about the future.

After my recent graduation from school I want to test my wings with a trip out into the world, before I try to realize my great dream. I want to gain recognition as a photographer, so that I can earn my living that way, or at any rate work in some way with illustrations and graphic design. I am aware that there is tough competition and that there are not many women who succeed. But I am thinking of fighting to achieve what I want.

Madeleine

Fredrik

*'Neighbours crossed over to the other side of the
road when they saw one of us coming.
It seems that they were afraid of grief.'*

Fredrik was born in 1987.
He was 13 years old when he lost his father, Christer.
(Fredrik's older sister, Caroline, tells her story on page 85.)

My childhood was like any other Swedish child's and I have had Mum and Dad at my side throughout all my ups and downs.

From my birth until the age of eight I lived in a suburb south of Stockholm. Then we moved to another suburb that is perfect for families with children, to a housing estate, close to the school and the centre. But I hated big changes when I was younger and found it difficult to adapt to new things. After a while I found some friends and I still have strong ties with them, which just get better and better.

My relationship with Dad was always good. We spent a lot of time together without any difficulties at all between us. He sat on the stands at the ice-hockey rink when I trained there and he and I played golf together. In our family we have always been very dependent upon each other. It was always the four of us. When Dad fell ill with leukaemia he said that it must be the punishment for having lived so happily together all the time.

During his last summer we had time to have our own holiday, just the two of us. We went to a little country town and spent all day every day on the golf course, ate at the hotel and had a very nice room. That is a wonderful memory now.

I shut myself off after Dad's death. Withdrew into myself for seven or eight months. Often had no energy to go to school. Didn't think there was any point in getting up. Thought that I wanted to die. Why hadn't I died instead, I thought. I didn't consider suicide at all, but I never dared to talk to Mum about this.

Mum, Sis and I tiptoed round each other and found it hard to share our grief. Two friends, a generally empathic boy and a friend whose mother had had breast cancer, have helped me a lot. Both are two years older than me.

My hockey coach gave Mum a bearhug and promised to look after me very well when Dad died. He had seemed rather cold at first. We found out that he had lost a child to leukaemia and he felt full of empathy for us.

But several of our neighbours turned their backs on us, looked away and crossed over to the other side of the road when they saw one of us coming. It was only when they were a bit drunk that they asked how we were getting on. Asked each other! As we found out. Not us. It seems that they were afraid of grief. But I wonder how they themselves would want to be treated if they were sad. 'Imagine if they start crying,' somebody had said in his own defence. My sister and I have been taught to behave towards others as we would like them to behave towards us, and it was a relief to move away from the house, the area and all the memories and to make a new start.

Two and a half years after Dad had died we moved to another house in another suburb.

Now there are just Mum and me at home. My sister has finished sixth form college and is reading Spanish in Barcelona to learn to stand on her own two feet.

I am attending the sports college and when Sis comes back from Spain she wants to move in at home again. I miss her a lot: the closeness.

I want to be in this book as a way of holding on to my memories. I am afraid of losing them. I notice already that I do not remember everything that has happened. My project in the fifth form was about grief. Unfortunately I did not save that essay. But Sis's essay on the same subject has given me a lot and is the best I have read about grief.

Fredrik

Felicia

'All the tubes were very scary,
but Mummy helped me to rub
body lotion into Daddy's skin.'

Felicia was born in 1995.
When she was six years old she lost her father, Christer.
(Felicia's older sister, Fanny, tells her story on page 77.)

I was sad when my daddy died.

He died of testicular cancer on 22 December 2000.

I went to visit him a lot at the hospital. At first it was alright to see him but then he was put on a respirator. All the tubes were very scary, but Mummy helped me to rub body lotion into Daddy's skin.

On Lucia Day me and my sister wanted to dress up and sing some Lucia songs for him. They let us even though he was in intensive care. I sang the Saint Lucia song and a Christmas song.

After he had died our mummy let us go with her to decide how we wanted the funeral to be. What flowers there would be on the coffin. Red roses shaped like a heart, one for each of us. I had a pink rose in my hand, which I lay down on it.

Felicia

Pontus

'I want other people to behave as if nothing has happened. I don't want anyone to ask anything.'

Pontus was born in 1993.
He lost his mother, Ulla-Carin about six months ago.

Mummy had a nerve disease called ALS. She died of it after about a year.

Mummy was very kind, probably the best mother in the world. When I was younger and it was her presenting the news on TV I used to run over and kiss her on the screen. It was kind of fun to see her there.

We had a good time together. And we did lots of things like going to the cinema and swimming at various pools. We went out into the country-side and fished and picked mushrooms and played laser games. Mummy arranged a lot of parties. When we were living in Canada (I went to school there) we went on a whale safari. We also had a trip to the USA although we mostly travelled around Canada. In New York we went up into the World Trade Centre just before it fell down. We also talked a lot, Mummy and I.

Last year when I was in the fourth grade and Mummy had fallen ill a lot of people came up to me and asked a lot of questions about it. I just used to say: 'I have to go and play football now.'

The newspapers wrote things that caused a misunderstanding and some people we knew thought that she was already dead and started ringing us up.

Mummy was at home all the time. I think that was a good thing. Though there were so many people here. Some were here to help her and sometimes new ones arrived. Some came over to fix all the equipment and then there were the people from Home Care. But we got used to it. Some of them became our friends.

A vicar came to our house and sang a song that Mummy liked a lot, about a beach. She had all of us around her. But most of all I would have liked it to have been just us, the family.

Mummy died at 12 o'clock, when I was at school. To see the coffin and to see my mother in it was sad, but not scary. I put my football in there with her. I would probably have been angry when I was grown-up if they hadn't let me see Mummy and be with her when she was dead. It wasn't scary, I promise. Even if I felt extra sad, it was worth it.

At six o'clock all of us in the family went with Mummy to a chapel where she was going to lie until the funeral.

The day after when I arrived at school everyone stared at me. A teacher asked if it was alright for them to mention it: 'Shall we talk about this situation or pretend that nothing has happened?'

If people aren't told about it straightaway then there will just be all the more gossip. When they had talked about it, everyone behaved as usual again.

The only thing I remember about Mummy's funeral is the photographers. They came rushing up to us and took photos of the coffin. Outside they had a car with its engine running. I think that it was weird that they couldn't leave us in peace. It was our business. It was clearly private. I have kept those newspapers. The things in them are so ugly. That sort of thing should be against the law.

Getting on with life

The worst of it is that you miss out on so much. She is not here and sometimes I just can't believe it.

Dad and I talk about Mummy. And I talk to her. Not aloud in words like on the telephone but more thoughts. Sometimes Dad asks if I want to go and visit her grave. But I don't think that is necessary. I can talk to Mummy at home.

I want other people to behave as if nothing has happened. I don't want anyone to ask anything except the family and Mummy's best friend, who helped her all the time. The worst thing that could happen now is if Dad died. When he had the flu I tried to help him all I could.

I wanted to start going to a cookery course but that autumn there was nothing for children. Only 'Gentlemen's Relish', a course for older men, and I didn't feel so interested in that.

I want things to be as usual. They never will be ever again, but everything else must be as it used to be. Though now we don't do as much as when Mummy was alive. I play tennis and football. I think sport helps because then I don't think about it as much.

We are making a few small changes in our house. We have got rid of the ramps and wheelchairs and stairlift that reminded us of Mummy's illness. Now we can remember more easily what she was like when she was healthy.

My younger brother and I have been given a more powerful computer with space for all our games, and a new TV. We have new wallpaper in our rooms and we're going to have new curtains.

What I would like most of all is for Dad and us to go canoeing and travel to Thailand or England. It is also fun when we go and visit our grown-up sisters.

Pontus

Fanny

*'We visit Daddy's grave on Father's Day with
chocolate and drawings for him. We took
a little glass of whisky to him on Christmas Eve.'*

Fanny was born in 1993.
She lost her father, Christer, when she was eight years old.
(Fanny's younger sister, Felicia, tells her story on page 71.)

When I got to know that my father had fallen ill I thought, I wonder what is going to happen. When we visited Daddy at the hospital it was alright. Though I think it was awful to see all the tubes. On Lucia Day we sang Lucia songs and rubbed body lotion on him. He died two days before Christmas Eve. When Mummy told us that Daddy had died I was as sad as anything. The funeral went well but I did not want to go in at first because I was afraid. It felt nice to get back to school. Everyone was very surprised when I told them, because nobody knew about it except my best friends. Me, our mother and my little sister Felicia take more care of each other nowadays.

Worst of all is not being able to meet Daddy. I miss talking to him and hugging him.

We visit Daddy's grave on Father's Day with chocolate and drawings for him. We go there on his birthday with birthday cards and flowers. We took a little glass of whisky to him on Christmas Eve.

Fanny

Magnus

'It was beautiful in there, peaceful.
He was lying there and he had a rose.'

Magnus was born in 1986.
He was 15 years old when he lost his father, Håkan.

Dad died on 28 March 2002 at a petrol station.

He had been away in another county to collect his new Yamaha Bulldog and he was driving it home. He ran out of petrol, knew the area, knew where there was a petrol station and pushed his motorbike to it. It was quite warm and he had his leather suit on. According to someone who worked there he put the bike on its stand and then he collapsed. He did not suffer.

I was told at about seven in the evening, when I was out with my friends. Mum rang me on my mobile and said: 'Come home, I want to talk to you.' When I got home two policemen and a vicar were standing in the kitchen, but Mum didn't want them to say anything. She took me into a room and didn't hesitate, just said it straight out.

It didn't feel as though I wanted to cry. It was too unreal, wasn't happening, not really, so there was nothing to cry about. Then they let me talk to the vicar. The police didn't say much.

Mum went to see Dad's mother but I didn't want to go with her. I went to a friend's home, a girl. But first I had to ring one of my friends to say why I hadn't come back. Then only ten minutes passed before the mobile started ringing: 'We don't know what to say,' they said, 'but we just wanted you to know that we're here for you.' It didn't matter at all that they didn't know how to say it.

That was that day.

It was the first day of the Easter holidays so I could stay at home and not go to school.

The next day we took the car down to the petrol station, Mum and I, Mum's sister and her husband. It was good to have a picture of what it looked like. They didn't know very much, but one girl who worked there had seen it. Then we went to the hospital, only Mum and I. The others waited outside. I didn't want to at first, but it was a good thing that I went in with her. I think it's easier when you see that it has really happened. It's easier to understand. I wanted to remember that happy man, but my brother persuaded me: 'You'll remember "that happy man" even if you see him now. Even though it's very hard you'll win in the long run if you do it.'

It was beautiful in there, peaceful. He was lying there and he had a rose. The motorcycle suit had arrived at our home in a bag. A very nice vicar and a nurse helped us to get ready in a nearby room before we went in, and they asked us afterwards how it had felt. The vicar went in with us. I stood a little way away and just looked, but I did not want to go up close.

During the time that followed my brothers and our relatives came home to us and did the cooking. I am the only child my parents have in common, although I have three older brothers and a sister. Dad's children, my brother and my sister, and Mum's two sons were here a lot.

As soon as we weren't with relatives and as soon as Mum was busy doing something, I rang my friends. It felt good to get away from home, good to have a change of company. We often talked about what had happened when we had just met up: 'How're things?' 'That's bad.' They sympathized a little and then I was able to talk about other things.

It takes a long time to understand what has happened. Okay, my father has died. It feels like nothing, as though it hasn't happened. It has sunk in bit by bit.

I went back to school after the holidays. Sometimes I went home after lunch and other times I simply couldn't go there at all. Mum had rung the school. 'Heard what happened, I'm so sorry, it must be hard,' they said, and I said: 'Can we talk about something else?' I didn't want to make it seem bigger than it was, a lot of people had nothing to do with it, but friends that I hadn't seen for one and a half years rang me and that was a positive thing. A girl who was one of my best friends sent me flowers. She liked Dad a lot. They had got on very well together since she was five or six years old, and she was very sad.

Mum said: 'Of course you must bring a good friend to the funeral if you like.' There was only one person I wanted to come, so that it wouldn't only be relatives and Dad's workmates. My friend sat all on his own, right at the back, but when we walked round the coffin he came up and hugged me and Mum. It was him I rang that evening. He has always been one of my closest friends.

That was in the church. I didn't help out with anything at all. Mum and Dad's workmates kept a better check on things. It was a good thing that everybody had the chance to say farewell and that they all had their few moments there by the coffin. Even those who did not know Dad that well. Everyone at the funeral went and had coffee and sandwiches afterwards in the church dining room.

When it was all over I went home to a friend's. It was very important for me to shut it all out. It had been sad, sad, sad, but now I was going to watch football. It's a case of finding a balance. Funerals wear you out. Everyone is sad and it is mentally exhausting. I had attended the funeral of one of Mum's best friends, so I knew what happened.

I sometimes think that I ought to spend time with Mum, but she has encouraged me when I've wanted to go out. She has done the same, but it took longer for her. To begin with she was at home, only at home, all the time. 'Can't you ring somebody, or meet somebody?' I asked, but she just thought it sounded like too much of an effort. In the end she realized that she had to. You have to get out, get back to school, start training, the lot.

Little things make you sad. I'm walking along in the street and I see a guy on a motorbike far away in the distance. I stop and watch until he has passed me. I often see someone who looks like Dad. I know that it isn't him of course, but it could be him. I can be walking along the pedestrian precinct and see him 18 times before I reach home, because I so want it to be him.

Dad as a person was happy and funny, though not with stand-up humour, exactly, but he was always wanting to find stuff to do. 'Shall we go for a ride on the motorbike?' Always home at five preparing the dinner. Mum worked until six and I sat there in the kitchen yelling for food. He did my homework with me before we ate, or afterwards.

But I didn't do as well at school and wasn't as good at sports as Dad had been, and spent nights out, so there was a lot of scolding. I was about 14. But I was never given a scolding without having earned it.

One has to be honest and do one's best to succeed at whatever one has set out to do. If one is at school then one has to succeed at school too. If one starts with a sport one must train hard. Said Dad.

The day that I am too tired to train is the day that I might just as well stop. It is from Dad that I have learnt never to do things by halves. To commit myself 100 per cent to something and not just 80.

Dad was a lawyer in labour legislation. Very competent and much appreciated, so it is a huge, wicked loss for the lawyers as well, I was told. But it had a price too. He was often tired and even got depressed. In the wintertime he always got rather grouchy and grumpy. I've inherited this. We should have travelled abroad during the winter, but we did that in the summertime – when I wanted to be at home.

We wanted to go on the motorbike down through Europe, to France, Italy… Now I want to buy a motorcycle, mostly because of Dad. He showed me how lovely it was, that there are other roads than motorways.

I have always been able to talk about Dad's death, but have heard about others who get angry and hit people to get it out of their system. I coach small guys under 13 in American football and I myself play in the Under Nineteens and with the seniors.

I get rid of my aggression through sport, I've noticed, and it takes a lot to make me angry. I am as calm as anything and totally in harmony with myself after training sessions. I used to be a try-this-and-that type of person. I tried floorball for kind of two months, football once and that was it… Nowadays the team and the coach have become a bit like a family for me.

The coach has been my Spanish teacher since the sixth grade and one of my friends had played in the team for two or three years. 'Cool! Welcome,' they said, and I'm going to become good… I'd rather be busy playing football all week than just drifting around. My coach coaches me for free, so I want to give something back to the younger ones – so that it spreads, and they might start coaching even younger players.

My relationship with Dad's older children is better and I've become an uncle to a little girl, and that is great.

I often go to the memorial grove at the graveyard, with the headstones round in a ring. In the middle there is a little stone circle with a fountain. Sometimes I sit down there and talk straight to Dad instead of going home and talking to Mum.

Just before he died he and I had spent time for several days chatting about problems of attitude, and we had just sorted it all out. Now I attend a carpentry college and I'm happy there.

Some time ago Mum felt a lump in her breast. She invited my brothers to dinner and said: 'I'm not worried, so I don't think you should be either.' But of course, why shouldn't it happen to us? Two of my friends had mothers with breast cancer, so it's not something that only happens to me. The lump was only five millimetres big when the doctor took it out, but I had time to think: Oh no, please not that too. But it was safe.

Mum has asked if I want to go to a social officer or a psychologist. The vicar who buried Dad and who is also my old vicar from my confirmation has said that we can sit and talk a bit, but I'm not much for sitting and talking. 'It's nothing personal, but I prefer talking to a friend who knew Dad rather than to you,' I said to my vicar.

Magnus

Caroline

*'It sounds easier than it actually is to talk
to a dying person about death.'*

Caroline was born in 1984.
When she was 16 years old she lost her father, Christer.
(Caroline's younger brother, Fredrik, tells his story on page 67.)

When I was 16 my father fell ill with leukaemia. Since he was a stubborn person, he battled against it for ten months before he died.

To help myself I wrote and read all through the worst times, while it was too sensitive for me to talk about it.

I found some stories that were useful to me in the textbook I had in Swedish. A short story about Sara who received a book six months before the death of her mother that she only read a long time afterwards. The book was *Death Is of Vital Importance* by Elisabeth Kübler-Ross. It says how important it is to talk about death and not to try and protect each other by not doing it. Sara regrets that she did not read the book while her mother was still alive, because in it were the answers to many of her questions.

The story had such a strong effect on me that I bought the book and it is the book that has touched me most. But it sounds easier than it actually is to talk to a dying person about death, because one does not want to confess that one is starting to lose hope. It feels like a betrayal that one even has thoughts that the outcome might not be good. There is a lot that one does not see, does not want to see, while it is happening, as my poems to Dad no doubt show.

> You said that you found sunsets upsetting.
> For you they were an invitation to a conversation you dreaded.
> I do not even remember what I answered.
> I did not understand then and I will not get a second chance.

> You cried but I did not understand.
> You faded away, but still I did not understand.
> Now you have gone, and I am starting to see.

After his death it was hard for me to stop thinking that he would be coming home any moment now. I found it hard to get rid of his stuff and refused to let Mum throw away his clothes. It was one of the few times we did not agree. Mum felt that she needed to clear out all traces of Dad so that she could get on with her life. In retrospect I sometimes think that it might perhaps have been better if we had done that, and perhaps I would not have had the feeling that he might come home at any moment. But at that time I needed the comfort of being able to go to his cupboard, lean inside it and hug the clothes that were hanging there, sniff them a little and almost feel that I was hugging Dad.

Goodbye Grandma by Louise Boije af Gennäs was another story in my textbook at sixth form college. It took me several attempts to get through it without bursting into tears. I recognized myself in the story and it meant a lot since it showed me that others react like me.

What I was most afraid of was that Dad would be in pain when he died. For that reason it was important for me to be with him when he slipped away, to be able to hold his hand and see that he was not in pain. I have a friend whose father died of a heart attack so suddenly that she did not have a chance to say farewell. When I think about her I feel great thankfulness for the year we were given to get used to the idea that Dad was not going to survive, even if I kept on hoping until the very end.

In the Unicef magazine I read about 17-year-old Annett in Uganda. The article had the rather pompous title 'Teenage girl with personal responsibility.' Her parents had died of AIDS two years before. She looks after five younger siblings and even succeeds in saving a little money for her youngest sister who she thinks is HIV-positive.

Annett inspires me. We were the same age when I read about her and wondered whether I too could be the head of a family. Yes, in fact it is something that I think everybody would manage to do. That is the way I have been brought up, to believe that I can do anything if I have the right attitude and work hard. I am impressed by Annett. Despite the pain of losing both her mother and her father she still manages to carry on with her life, be a role model and support her family.

Our family has survived quite well, but my younger brother and I have lost a few years of our childhood. We had to grow up and have learnt to manage on our own for the most part. But Mum will always be Mum.

The feeling of loss is there in lots of ways. Sometimes I miss having Dad to discuss things with, sometimes I miss romping around with him, sometimes it is having Dad feel proud of me and sometimes even having

Dad scold me. I wonder very often what Dad would have thought or said. I believe that most people who have lost a relative or close friend go around wondering what the dead person would have thought or done. You can't just shut off everything that had to do with him or her.

In my family we were unable to grieve together. The three of us who were left behind and who were expected to get on with our lives disappeared in different directions. Away from the empty chair at the dining table, away from old habits, away from the traces he left. We have coped with it in our own individual ways.

I remember the evening that we were told that Dad was ill. Dad had stayed at the hospital and the rest of us went home. Mum rushed straight in and rang Granny; she was wailing and crying. My brother shovelled snow in the drive in the middle of a snowstorm, he shovelled and shovelled away for hours, inconsolable. I went into my room, put out the light and lay down curled up like a foetus.

I withdrew inside myself during the time after his death and was unable to talk to anyone. The sleeping problems that I already had became more serious. I kept myself occupied all the time to keep the thoughts away. I suffered from burn-out at school and had a cold for one week each month since my body was too tired to carry on as usual.

As a grieving child I have been left to my own devices, with my loneliness, fear and shame. I do not want to show how bad I feel; I prefer nobody to know about it. This is to protect myself and also to make things easier for others. At the same time I hope that somebody will ring and ask how I am or make me come out with them even if I usually do not want to. It is important that those who ring do not give up, because I do not ring, do not want to be a nuisance. I just want to know that I am not completely alone.

I felt ashamed when the neighbours turned away, out of fear I suppose. It is imprinted in my memory. That people who were recently our friends did not greet us, ask us how we were or even look in our direction. I felt as though I had the plague. What had we done wrong?

Nowadays I can understand that fear. But one does not have to talk about death or chemotherapy – it is alright to talk about the weather. Imagine if someone had picked a bunch of flowers and handed it to us personally, instead of sending flowers by messenger. Or knocked on the door with a pot of bolognese sauce, so that we had been able to eat homemade food one evening, since Mum seldom had the time or energy. Perhaps offered to mow the lawn. Anything at all, it is so simple.

After less than a year I started going to a psychologist, but it took time to find the right one. It is not easy to open up to a stranger, trust somebody you have never met before, but it is possible. The first one I ended up with was able to sit in silence for several minutes; it felt as though she was searching for comforting words to say and I felt ashamed of making her feel so uncomfortable. Another one made me tell her what I had gone through without asking any questions and since I was much too uncertain and feeling too unhappy I could not cope with it at all. The woman that I at last dared to tell everything to (I think she was the sixth) knew how to get me to talk, knew that I needed help to dare. I visited her for six months and on my last visit we were able to make jokes about how I had changed. From sitting hunched up and only answering questions to coming into the room, throwing myself into the armchair and telling her how my week had been.

I was now ready to let Mum empty Dad's wardrobe. I no longer needed his stuff close to me and I was able to get on with my life.

'We lost our zest for life afterwards' was a title in the magazine *Children and Cancer* that caught my attention. A father tells the story of what the family's life was like when it was at its worst after their four-year-old daughter had contracted cancer. He talks about the incredible tiredness that overwhelmed them when the doctors had killed the tumour and saved their daughter. I know all about that tiredness, even though my father was never cured and my tiredness only appeared after Dad had died. In fact it is hard to describe, one probably has to have experienced it. It is both physical and mental and so deep that it hurts. A whole year of held-back, hidden anger, grief and fear bloomed into a tiredness that I tried to describe in this way:

> To stand up though you are broken,
> To smile though it hurts,
> To live though you do not dare,
> That is courage.

Three and a half years have passed now since Dad died.

I fled to Barcelona straight after sixth form college. I thought that it would be easier to get on with my life in a new place, with a new language and new impressions. But here I am a year later, wiser in many ways, but still grieving.

I have heard so many amazing life stories and have several times sat with somebody I hardly know who has been through something similar and cried together. Somebody who knows exactly what it feels like to lose someone close to you, and that has helped me. But it has taken me three years to get to the point where I can talk about Dad and laugh instead of cry. I am so proud of myself. Dad is too, I know it.

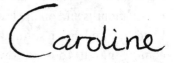

Ismail

*'It sometimes feels like my fault that he
was killed. I did not stop him from
going and taking part in that war.'*

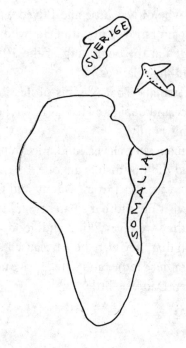

Ismail was born in 1985.

He was ten years old when he lost his father, Muse.

A sad moment

The worst and saddest moment I have ever had in my life was when I got to hear that my father had been killed in a civil war in Somalia.

I was born in Somalia, in a town called Burao.

I am now in my final year studying science at a sixth form college and I live in a suburb of the capital of Sweden. I have lived there for six years with my mother, my stepfather and my sisters and brothers. When I have graduated I want to work for a year and move to a flat with a friend and give football a try. If that does not work out I want to study economics, living in a student hostel, and become a businessman like Dad.

My parents divorced when I was little and I lived with Mum. But when my mother married again I moved in with Dad, who had also remarried. Mum moved to Sweden at the beginning of the 1990s and I stayed in Somalia with Dad and my relatives.

Dad was a businessman. That was his profession. We had a small company that sold rice and bananas. He was not at home very often, but always had time for his family.

Dad was a gentleman: very clever, kind, nice, reliable and ambitious. He liked everyone and did not dislike anyone. I have never met anyone who was as nice as he was, apart from Granny and Grandad.

I used to go and visit my mother's parents and stay for a long time. The reason was that they were very kind and good to me and everyone else. Sometimes I wish that they were here because I long for them. Then I used to go on to my father's father and sister. I have never met his mother because she died when Dad was little.

Life in Somalia

My life in Somalia was a good one. We were a happy family. I did not go to school but used to go to lectures that were a bit like school. But at school you learn a mass of subjects. At the lectures we only learnt about religion with the Koran as our textbook.

My father was a very good dad who supported his family and looked after us. He always wanted the best for his family. He was an open person who used to talk to me about what was right and wrong. One could say that we had a good relationship, as I had with my whole family.

Dad was killed in 1995, in a civil war that was being fought just where we lived, in Burao.

When my mother heard what had happened she arranged for me and my little brother to come and live with her in Sweden.

When I came to Sweden

My younger brother and I arrived in Sweden at the end of 1997. Everything was so new to me. It was as though I had arrived in another world. I saw masses of white people and had never seen so many before.

Mum and her husband fetched us from the plane at Stockholm Airport. Mum's husband is now my stepfather and he is very kind and decent.

At present

At present I am a student and I play football almost every day after school. My interest is football and I love it. I play a lot in my spare time and go to football practice. When I'm not playing football or doing homework I'm hanging out with my friends.

I do not ever want to move back to Somalia to live there, but I would like to go there on holiday. I want to live here for ever. You can't trust Somalia. It is full of risks. War can break out there at absolutely any moment and that is why I do not want to move back there.

I have been without a father now for a long time and I don't cry any longer when I think about him. I often used to cry when I was younger. When I think about Dad now I also think about things that he taught me, like fishing for example.

It sometimes feels like my fault that he was killed. I did not stop him from going and taking part in that war. But all human beings are going to die, and this beautiful world is not going to last for ever, so I have had to accept that it was not my fault.

I have no photo to look at when I remember him. We do not have them in my culture. But in Somalia they bury people as they do in Sweden. I used to visit Dad's grave there almost every day.

A nice moment
The best moment I have had was when I saw Mum for the first time for several years. Saw her standing there with a lovely smile waiting for us at Stockholm Airport.

ISmail

Saga

*'Every time I look at myself in the mirror I stare into
my own eyes and seek out Daddy's gaze.'*

Saga was born in 1985.
She lost her father, Hans, when she was ten years old.

The evening before. Mummy and I are standing together on a street corner. Behind us a display window is radiating light and the street lights are twinkling, but otherwise the evening is calm and quiet. Light snow flakes are falling to the ground. I am happy and expectant and my feet are tired. We have been out to hire slalom equipment because we are going up into the mountains, to meet our cousins and ski.

Now everything is ready – we have bought everything and packed everything. Mummy is talking to Daddy on the mobile phone. He is only going to work for a little longer, and then he will be coming home. We are like that. We pack, shop, pack a bit more, and always get away one or two days later than we originally intended. That is the way things should be. That is the way they have always been.

I look up at the office where Daddy works. He has the room at the top of the building, with the big window. It is the only room with the light on now. Then I see a dark silhouette raising its arm and waving. It is Daddy. He is up in his room and is only going to work for a little while longer. Mummy and I are down here on the street corner. In a way he is very far away – just a little dark shadow – but in a way he is really so close. I can hear his voice on the mobile.

When one's father dies the whole world collapses. Everything becomes black, irreversibly black.

Life becomes a big black hole, a nightmare. At night I lie tossing and turning in bed, and repeat the words 'Never, ever, ever again…'. I will never, ever, ever see him again.

At first it is not so bad. Things like this do not happen to me. They happen to people in books, in newspapers, but not to me. He has only fainted, it is nothing to worry about.

Then, slowly, fear starts to force itself on me. There is something that is really, really wrong. When I am honest with myself I realize it. I feel it in Mummy's voice, in the looks other people give me. The air is so heavy. Telephone signals jangle through the house.

A long night arrives when I just lie and stare out into the darkness. I toss and turn. Stare down into that black hole that has been torn in the middle of reality. I taste the irreversible. Daddy is dead. Dead, dead, dead.

The world turns strange. It is naked and cold, distorted and waveringly unreal. In everyone's faces I see uncertainty and fear lurking under the skin. It is upsetting to meet, upsetting to talk, upsetting merely to exist.

We are at the hospital, everything is white. People are kind, people send letters and tulips. But nothing matters. Everything has been destroyed. It is never, ever, ever going to be as it should be again. Never. Ever.

We are going to see Daddy before the funeral. The doctor has said that this is a good thing. So that I will really understand that he is dead. We enter a dark, bare room, and I am terribly scared. It feels embarrassing too, with all the other people around us.

On a stretcher in the middle, covered by a white sheet so that only his head is visible, lies a man. He is pale and cold. On his forehead he has a few small cuts where the blood has hardened into scabs. I stand and look at him. It is not Daddy. It is a stranger, an empty shell, a doll. There is nothing left of Daddy there. My cousin cuts off a lock of hair for me. It is Daddy's hair, but it is not Daddy. I have left my real daddy in the car after the accident. He will never come back to me.

He does not exist, I explain to myself. I say it over and over again, and it is as if the whole of me is being torn to pieces. I curl up like a foetus and can feel in my stomach how I am being torn apart, chewed up from inside. Daddy and I belong together. He has been cut away. A part of me has been amputated.

My grief is totally selfish. I want to have Daddy here with me. My whole world is built on his being there for me, as he always has been and always should be.

A long time ago

We are in a pedestrian tunnel with yellow tiles. Mummy and I are going to meet Daddy and we have been apart for a long time, certainly a whole week. We come walking along from one end, and we glimpse Daddy far away at the other end. My longing for him is so powerful that it is tugging at my stomach. I run towards him through the tunnel and throw myself up into his arms. There is a crashing sound as his thick brown spectacles fall off and are broken to pieces against the stone floor. They break into at least 20 pieces. Well, ten anyway. But Daddy just laughs. He hugs me, laughing.

Mummy laughs too, every time she sees him drive the car. Because Daddy and I collected all the pieces of his spectacles and when we got home he taped them together. Now he uses them as car spectacles. They work just as well as before – although he doesn't really look all there.

The feeling in my stomach now is the same as then. Something is tearing and tugging at me inside, demanding that I rush off and throw myself into his arms. But I will never be able to do that. Daddy is no longer there to catch me.

I don't believe at all that Daddy is grieving for himself, if it is at all possible to think in that way. He was always calm. Nothing went against him. If Daddy died then even death had to listen to his gentle voice and his objective arguments, and admit that Daddy was right of course. Therefore it is mostly me who should be pitied. Mummy and me. We are the ones who have been left behind.

The thing that has become most important is to keep him close by me. The worst times are when I feel that he is slipping away from me, that he is slipping further and further away. I left my real daddy with his dark curly hair in the car when I got out. I tramped away through the snow and the shattered glass and left him there.

Now the daddy that I must keep close by me is the daddy that I have inside me. It is the image of him on the inside of my eyelids, the feeling of hugging him, his voice. I shut my eyes tightly and try to make him appear, so that I can see that he will stay with me for ever and ever. I write letters to him, talk, ask, nag – anything to stop the contact between us from being broken off, anything to stop him from disappearing.

I create my own rituals. Every time I look at myself in the mirror I stare into my own eyes and seek out Daddy's gaze. I stare and stare, and in the end it is Daddy that I see. Then I know that he is still here inside me.

We are travelling by car. I am looking up at the clouds, or out over the treetops, and if I concentrate I can feel that Daddy is there, as a part of the world, still here with me.

I know that I have hugged him, I know that I have looked into his eyes, I know that his genes are in me. His hugs must therefore still be inside me. His image must therefore still be on my retina. That's why he is still alive in me.

We collect his clothes together, Mummy and I. We take the sheets of paper that he has doodled on, the pillowcase that he slept on, the tape with his voice on in the answering machine, and we put it all in a large cardboard box. All these things are important, because they are going to help me to keep him close to me.

These things are important at first, but after a while I feel that they are not necessary. Then I discover that I am no longer afraid. Daddy is still there. He has been so important to me that it is impossible for him ever to disappear or fade away. I might perhaps forget his voice, I might perhaps forget the way he smelled. But that does not matter. Everything that we have done, everything that we have said; it is all still there inside me. Whenever I feel like it I can look up at his window and see his silhouette waving at me. He is still close to me, but I can no longer throw myself into his arms.

Saga

Gustaf

'During the last years of your life you gave me all I need. You died sober! I'm very proud of you.'

Gustaf was born in 1984.
He lost his mother, Kerstin, when he was 18 years old.

I thought that Mum was just being bloody-minded when she drank, until I understood that alcoholism is an illness and can often run in families, and I believe that even Dad is an alcoholic (I know the bloke's name and where he lives, but have never met him). So it is in my genes and I run quite a big risk too. But I have chosen not to drink at all. I don't think it tastes good and I would hate to lose control, get drunk and have a hangover.

My ma – by the grace of God – cottoned on to the idea that she needed help, after a lot of ifs and buts. A very good alcoholism therapist gave her a leaflet on the symptoms of the illness, which said that even the family dog can be affected if anybody at home is an alcoholic. Ma realized that, okay, I fit this description, and at long last she realized that she had no alternative but to stop drinking.

Mum was a very good teacher and always managed to get to school. She was liked by the children and she was an excellent pedagogue.

She received help from her school to go into a special home for a month's treatment. Later on I went there for a family week. It was really good to be able to talk about it and I learnt a lot. I used to try and help Mum by lying: 'No, Mum doesn't drink.' Shit, it was tough going. Looking after Mum, saving Mum; that was my role and it has made me very aware about helping others. Mum started going to AA meetings, and I joined a self-help group for teenage relatives. Now I attend an adult group.

Mum as a sober person was very different and she started to get a grip on what life was all about. I was 16 at the time and had left home and was living at a friend's and with a foster family. However, when I heard that she was sober and was working on herself, I started seeing her and, after a few weeks, I moved back home again.

Things had always been chaotic at home but all of a sudden it was clean and neat, with fruit and sweets in bowls on the table. Mum laid out breakfast for me. There was a nice smell and the sound of classical music.

Mum wrote personal reflections in her diary and squeezed oranges. What a change, it was totally freaky.

Of course I remember short periods earlier on when she was sober, but it was only now that our relationship became really good. We both worked on our behaviour patterns and it was super cool to spend time together as friends. I had escaped before, often to a friend who lived nearby. Some of my friends' parents had suspected how things were and let me stay at their place. Now Mum started welcoming my friends and letting them sleep over at our place.

What was so crazy about Mum's death was that our life had just started to be so good.

We were on holiday on an island that I have been to since I was little. We had dinner, Mum and I, and after the meal she told me that she had a slight pain in her stomach. I said, 'Oh, okay, but I'm going out to meet my friends.' When I came back home that night Mum was throwing up and groaning. Shit, I thought, what's all this? She was the type who never complained. 'Shit, Mum, what's wrong?'

'Yuck, I've got such a terrible stomach ache,' she replied, and then threw up over and over again.

Shit, what do we do now, on an island in an archipelago? Ring for an ambulance out here? She wanted to wait until six o'clock. Then I ran to the shop and got hold of a bloke who worked there. 'Something's wrong with Ma. She's feeling very sick.' He fetched her in his pickup truck and took her on the ferry to the nearest town. Such a bloody little hospital! There didn't seem to be anything advanced there. Mum thought she had a twisted intestine and I just…shit, okay, okay… They listened and palpated and decided to take Ma to a bigger hospital in an ambulance. Shit, what the hell was happening? I said the prayer for peace of mind to give myself strength and courage: 'God, give me peace of mind to accept what I cannot change, courage to change what I can and wisdom to understand the difference.'

The main hospital said it was a twisted intestine, but Mum was only allowed to stay for two nights. Perhaps other people needed the bed a lot more. Hospitals are disgusting. Illness clung to the walls and I didn't want to touch anything. I was dissatisfied with the way we were treated.

Back home she threw up again. Her sister and brothers came to visit her and we sent her to a smaller hospital that was not under so much pressure. She stayed there for quite a long time and was X-rayed. I could see the hospital from my school and I tried to spend as much time with her as possible. She wanted me to, but it was hard. I got angry at Mum because she became so pathetic and so childish, but you can't blame a person who has cancer.

I suppose I was just scared. They cut out six metres of her intestine when she had the operation! Practically pointless, because there was so much cancer. 'I'm not going to survive,' she said.

'Oh hell Mum, that's so sad, bloody hell.' Mum was unhappy and had tears in her eyes.

'I love you Mum.'

'I love you too,' she said.

The doctor came and explained in more detail what was going to happen: chemotherapy, tiredness, losing her hair. It fucking sucks. She could maybe even live for another six months.

What will happen to me when Mum dies?

We were a little family: my brother, Mum and I. My brother is, like, 15 years older and has always been kind of a dad to me: 'I'll try and look after you,' he said, as we were walking around the hospital talking about everything.

Mum was feeling a bit better. The doctor thought that it would be alright to travel to London in September. In August she was back home and I helped her. When we went out in town she had to sit down often, have a coffee and so on. But we had a very nice time.

It was my 18th birthday on 30 September 2002. A few days before that we flew to London. We had been there before, Mum, my brother and me, but it had been a disaster because Mum was not sober. Now we were making the trip again. Staying at the Regent Palace, right in Piccadilly Circus. Posh as hell, beautiful rooms. After a while there was a knock at the door. My brother had arrived on a later flight. It was just so flipping great and I was incredibly happy, because I love my brother. He is totally wonderful.

London is a great city. We ate at a Lebanese restaurant in China Town late in the evening, talked, strolled around in a special mood that hadn't

been there before, and every minute was really lovely. It had finally
dawned on us that now was the time to make the most of each other.

My brother had been very angry with Mum, but he had forgiven her
and they talked lots and lots. 'Oh no, now I have no energy left,' she
sometimes said. When she felt like that, my brother and I could go out in
London together and do just male stuff. Close to Piccadilly Circus there
was an amusement arcade with shooting and football games, free fall and
light diodes all over the place.

On my birthday they let me choose everything and so we went out to
Alperton, which is a suburb with only Indians and masses of shops selling
joss sticks and gods. I was given a little temple by my brother for my
Krishna to live in. We ate at Govinda's. On the upper floor there was a
beautiful temple room. My brother and I joined in the singing and
playing.

It was through Mum that I started to believe. When she became sober she
tried to find a higher power who she could ask for help. Mum was very
much an atheist and found it hard to accept Christianity, just like me.
Some say Krishna, others say God, Jahve, Allah – Mum just said 'My
higher power'. She used to read the Bhagavadgita with me and we discussed God and spirituality. You could be soft with Mum, talk about life
and have a damn good time. She wasn't afraid of dying. Okay, it is difficult to be, like, immune against death, but she never said: 'Yuck, I don't
want to talk about that.'

When we got home from London she started feeling worse again and she
went into a hospice for cancer sufferers who are nearing death. I stayed at
my brother's as he didn't want me to live alone in the flat.

It was bloody upsetting to be at the hospice. My brother often slept
over there and talked with Mum a lot and I tried to be there too. Mum had
more and more difficulty in breathing. She slept an awful lot and had got
so bloody thin. When I noticed that, thinking shit, this is probably the
end, I tried to meditate extra hard and to get help from my higher power.
Of course my philosophy is that we are our souls, not our bodies. Mum's

body was breaking down, but I believe what the second chapter of the Bhagavadgita says about the soul.

It isn't the end if Mum dies, I thought. She is just changing bodies. I felt so sorry for Mum and used to say: 'Don't forget that you are the soul. My brother and I will do alright, you don't need to worry.' But it was heavy, depressing and sad.

When my brother and I had to go back to his place for some sleep, the hospice said it would call us if Mum got worse. If she died. I dreamt that they rang and we did not get there in time. We were so tense all the time. One night they really did call us. My brother woke me and we got a taxi. Mum had woken up and was looking at the chair where my brother had been sitting. You could hear her breathing less frequently. I thought it was the end, thought 'shit,' but then there was another breath, then a little white mucus, and then a nurse said that she had left her body.

A relief for Mum to be set free. But what an enormous difference, there was only a body left behind...

I felt desolate. Who would look after us? We had hoped that someone would come along and tell us what we should do now. We decided to go somewhere to have a snack.

We went to Govinda's. When one goes into the temple one usually shows reverence, so I prostrated myself. I gave thanks that Mum had been set free and that it had been granted to me to be there when she died. Not everyone is given that privilege. Oh hell, it's so damn heavy and hard to understand.

Confusion. Hell, everything's mad. I was numb, but didn't cry, just felt a special strange calm, and tiredness. My brother, Mum's sister and I talked through everything. We had lunch and then went to a funeral parlour where they were damn decent.

She should be scattered over the sea, I thought. She has always loved the sea. A coffin, a headstone? They asked about a grave or an urn in a memorial garden. 'That's your business, you must decide,' I said to my brother, but thought that fuck, perhaps a grave is alright. He chose the grave and we selected the stone together. 'Kerstin' and two birds. Or perhaps the birds were in the obituary? Is it blasphemy not to remember what is on her stone? She herself would just have said: 'So what? You're doing your best.'

There is a lady vicar who I went to when I was going to be confirmed, only I never got confirmed. She had been following the changes in our family so of course we rang her.

There was a funeral. A hell of a lot of wreaths, masses of people. At school, Mum had just started with a class in the first grade and I got a terrific shock when a lot of children and parents turned up. I only cried a little. Not because I think it's unmanly. It is very beautiful to see people crying in public. Daring to show that one is sad is brave.

I made a speech of thanks to Mum: 'Thank you for all you have meant to me. I love you so much and during the last years of your life you gave me all I need. You died sober! I'm very proud of you.' As I see it Krishna gave Mum an extra chance: 'If you choose to become sober you will have time to put things right. Then you can go home.'

She became sober, got me back and made me love her in a way that I had not been able to love her before.

We had time to revisit all the places where there had been a disaster: Denmark, London, Turkey. When we arrived she said: 'Tell me if I said or did anything stupid here when I was drunk.' We went around and exchanged all the bad memories for good ones. So fucking much had happened in her life and she was ready. She had got her sons back, seen her grandchildren, been reunited with her family at last and had a whole new life.

When one prays to a higher power for help things do happen. 'Listen up, you higher power, I don't even know who you are or if you exist, but I need you now.' I really benefit from my belief in Krishna.

My brother and I have rows about my religion. He thinks it's crazy shit and I suppose he's afraid that I will disappear into it. It was so damn nice to have Mum as a wall to bounce ideas off. Now my brother and his family are a great support.

It's crazy, but good things have also happened since Mum died.

My brother got in touch with the social services so that I was given a contact person and she and I are very alike. She is young, about 30, as is her boyfriend. We three are totally in sync. Just try and get a flat in the Old Town if you dare! They helped me with that and they are there if I'm sad or just want to meet up. They gave me a hand in packing up Mum's flat and I'm just so incredibly grateful for that. It's wicked how many people have said 'Come and see me if things get hard, promise me that,' but I find it difficult to accept help.

Anyway, I went to see a social welfare officer. An old, slim lady, very, very wise. I visited her every week to talk before Mum died, but then I wanted to stop. That's how I felt then.

Now I periodically go through ups and downs. Fuck, Mum, now I've met a weird girl again, what shall I do? Mum had such a lot of wisdom inside her. 'That girl is no good for you,' she would say and I'd think: Fuck, Mum, how could you know that it isn't working? Or like this: Mum, a most amazing thing has happened to me, so damn cool, met a lovely person who you will like… 'Take it easy, one thing at a time,' Mum might answer to that, or 'Don't be so hard on yourself.' She could also get me going when I was just lazing around.

At first I wanted to work with food and kitchens, so in the eighth grade I trained at a lunch restaurant. 'Cut these up, 150 sausages! Crack these, 200 eggs! Then empty the floor drains!' Stress, stress.

My next training position was at a nursery school. Cute young girls with long nails worked there. They took good care of the children and their nails at the same time. They cared a whole damn lot. I was staying with a friend and looking for a foster family and one of those girls said that she would really like to look after me.

Now I myself am a children's nurse. Things have gone well. No failures, only passes and excellents in my report even though I have dyslexia. The school helped me by having the books read aloud.

Now and then I go to Mum's grave. Not because I know where she is now, but anything is better than that broken-down body. I have learnt that feelings are important. I am not going to shut my eyes to reality and I want to work on my grief. But at a calm pace, without forcing it.

Sometimes I forget to grieve.

Johanna

*'You lie down and die or you get on with your life,
and grow more serious and a bit more careful.'*

Johanna was born in 1991.
When she was nine years old she lost her mother, Susanne.

In my family things have never been really perfect, but who says they have to be? Everyone probably dreams about having a perfect family and I certainly dreamt about it.

A lot of the fighting at home was about me and how I should be brought up. Dad said no and Mum said yes when I yelled as all children do. They had quite different ideas.

My mother, Susanne, had shoulder-length dark-brown hair, blue-green eyes and was quite heavy but pretty. A very clever woman. She painted when she had the time, and her paintings were wonderful. They were mostly of flowers, but Mum also painted other subjects like me and friends.

She worked on projects for the railways, had a good salary and had always been clever. At school and otherwise too. 'You're so clever. You'll be best,' is what she had always been told.

At 16 she left home. I don't know very much about her childhood, unfortunately. She came from Finland but moved to Sweden early on in her life. She met Dad at a party, they fell in love, made a home together and then they had me.

Mum had lots of friends and was herself a really good friend, but should have thought more about her own needs than about others. She wanted to be the perfect wife and mother. Women always think they have to take care of everyone. I think that's wrong.

Mum was overweight, and therefore she very often didn't want to go out and be seen, and that was a pity. If she'd been alive today I would have wanted to try and help her with her weight problem.

Mum and I usually did nothing special together, well – she worked so hard and all that, which was a problem the whole family suffered from at times.

But on weekday mornings my father left early and Mum and I spent time together and used to listen to tapes, such as Disney and Astrid Lindgren stories, before it was time to go to work and school. We walked a little of the way together, because the stop where Mum took the bus to work was on my way to school. When school was over, I walked home alone or else I was fetched by Dad. Mum – Mum worked until six or nine in the evening.

At weekends we didn't do much. We painted sometimes and mostly spent time with friends. In the summer we sometimes went on a trip to an island or to our former neighbours' country cottage, or to my uncle and his wife's summer cottage.

Monday 27 March

The past year had been hectic and hard and I had lost my beloved rabbit. Mum had worked so much that it had left its mark on her, and the whole family suffered from it. She was burnt out. She was off sick and at home most of the time, couldn't sleep and at times felt very low.

That Monday Mum was going to do something or other in a nearby suburb, I remember. And at school there was a sports tournament. I was in the third year and had just turned nine.

That morning was as usual except that Dad didn't leave early. I was on my way to school and hugged Mum and Dad. What I didn't know then was that it was the last time I'd ever see Mum…

School was as usual, but just before it was my team's turn in the tournament, my aunt came into the gym. She is a very important person in my life. She always has been and she always will be.

In any case she came in and said that we were going somewhere. I went out with her and we left in her car. I didn't know where to. When I asked, she just said that we were on our way to Dad. I remember how happy I was because my aunt had come to fetch me so suddenly and unexpectedly. 'This is probably one of the best days of my life,' I said to her – completely unaware that it was quite the opposite…

At last we arrived at where we were going. I didn't know where we were but followed my aunt. We went to a reception desk. I didn't listen to what my aunt and the woman at the reception desk were talking about. I stood wondering what we were doing there. But I had no idea.

When they had finished talking, we started to walk. We came to a room and in it sat Dad on a chair. There was also a hospital bed in there. Then I started to have a vague inkling. I thought that perhaps Granny had been taken ill and died, since she was so old and had been close to death before.

We went up to Dad and he started talking. I didn't listen much to the words, but I heard him say that there had been a fire at our house and – the rest I worked out for myself.

'Is Mummy dead?' I said with tears in my eyes. The answer was like knives stabbing into my heart, and a great black hole opened up in my soul. Tears gushed out and blinded me. It took some time to get them to stop, though finally they stopped, but there was an ache in my chest – it was the shock.

That afternoon, four years ago, I didn't believe that life could continue.

But we had the consequences to deal with…

'Where are we going to live?' I gathered up my courage and rang our neighbours who lived opposite our fire-damaged house. It was from them we used to borrow a country cottage. Daddy told them what had happened. I asked if we could stay with them. The answer was yes. The word that had just hurt me so…

The first night was very hard. And telling our friends…

How had the fire started? It was only after several weeks that I began to understand. It was like a jigsaw puzzle. At last, all the pieces were in place except one. They let me read a letter that Mum had left, but I will not read it again. It was suicide. So she chose it herself. That felt easier than if it had been an accident. If that was what she wanted.

I returned to school after a month and was given a lot of presents by teachers and friends. And even by the fire brigade. A monkey in a fireman's uniform that I still have. The presents were mostly cuddly toys, like a little cuddly dog and a teddy bear. My old cuddly toys had been damaged by smoke. I was also given things that people had made themselves. One whole day was dedicated to me and people almost overdid it a bit.

The first period of time was incredibly hard. It takes time to realize that one will never ever meet a person again. Especially if it's your mother. It is frustrating and sorrowful never to be able to say the word 'Mummy' again.

I hate it when people ask 'How can you live without your mother? I couldn't.' I think the answer is clear, because one has no choice. One has to survive. But I really appreciated it when a boy from another class, whose locker is next to mine, said when we met at our lockers, 'You're really strong to have coped with all this stuff about your mother.' And we don't even know each other.

Either you lie down and die or you get on with your life, and grow more serious and a bit more careful, and it's hard not to be able to be a child for as long as you need to be.

Some days it feels as though life is never going to turn out well, other days it feels as though the sun has come out again, like after rain.

It was important to have a new home, to make a change and not just carry on in the same old way. We searched for a long time, but when we came into this flat I immediately felt that it was the right one and said 'Dad, this is where I want to live. We can start a new life here.'

I've gone to psychologists and the Child Guidance Clinic, and the Save the Children grief group, which has given me the most. Psychologists mostly sit and ask, 'How are you feeling now?'

What's important is never to let go, even if your fear is great. I feel a lot of fear that it will be the same for me as it was for Mum. I don't want to be 20 and think 'God, what's happened to me?' I don't want to be shut inside myself. It doesn't matter what it costs, you have to be alright.

At the Save the Children grief group you could have snacks, tell stories, talk, draw yourself, show where fear and crying sit in your body and draw thought-maps. The others sitting there are children who know what you're feeling. You can cry, you can laugh. The grown-ups only help out if you don't know what to say. But it took two years in the queue before I was allowed to join. I thought then that it was too late but went anyway. Now I've heard that the groups have been stopped because there's no money for them. That's awful. I've felt how cruel the world is.

I would have found it difficult to manage without the people around me and would very much like to thank people: Dad, my aunt of course, my uncle and his wife, my other uncle and his wife, my cousins (they're only small, it's true, but they cheer me up); Granny, and my friend, who had the same experience with her dad. She doesn't find it as easy to talk about it as I do, so I try to help her. Her mum is a bit like an extra mother for me. Then there are the family's friends and mine. My pretend grandad in Germany, that is, Granny's ex-husband and his wife. He is very kind and still cares about me and I think that's great. At my country cottage there's a neighbour who means a lot to me. A grown-up best friend, who is cool, understanding and like a mother.

And then I have my support family. I once said to Dad when we were having a row that I wanted to be adopted somewhere else, but he just said 'We can't carry on like this, Johanna. We'll have to do something about it.' We applied to the local council and were given a family as support every third week. They're my friends now. They live in a posh suburb in an enormous luxury villa and that is also something that I need.

I want to become an actress in the USA, but I don't believe I will succeed. Or something to do with animals. Perhaps an author, because I'm verbally well developed and that is a gift from God. But in any case I'm going to ensure myself a really good education.

Even if four years have passed since Mum died, the grief will probably always be there. The knife wounds in my heart have become scars but will never disappear. One has to find the right way to get through the most difficult times of all.

I still haven't found it, but life is moving in the right direction, following tiny little paths.

During these years I've learnt one thing: to make the most of each day as if it were the last and never to lose hope.

Yours,

Martin

'Don't be afraid of seeing grief-stricken
people cry. We are not angry at you. We are
feeling the loss of someone we love.'

Martin was born in 1984.
He was 14 years old when he lost his mother, Annelie.

My family had just moved house. We had left our home and packed everything in boxes. Left behind were only empty rooms. Dad had found a new job in a new town, filled with new people. So I would have to get to know everybody again. We had moved several times. But this time I didn't want to and I suffered. That was how my time at secondary school started.

I remember that I yelled at Mum. I didn't want to move. Thought it was wrong. Mum comforted me. Promised that everything would be alright, hugged me tightly. She thought I ought to go to a child psychologist. I went, unwillingly, and the psychologist let me cry as much as I needed, and it felt better.

Mum had started studying again. She was going to change her job. Get a qualification in public health science. She had been a midwife before. Statistics were included in the course. Neither Mum nor I understood the charm of equations, the figures meant nothing to us, ran into each other like porridge and were impossible to get a grip on.

When she became ill she carried on swotting in bed. She refused to give up, still hopeful. One day perhaps she would regain her health.

Mum had stomach cancer. An unusually aggressive kind. Now, afterwards, I find myself wondering why she didn't discover it earlier. She of all people must have noticed that something was wrong. But I suspect that she was too stubborn to admit that she was ill. Probably believed that it was impossible. Or that it would go away and that everything would turn out alright. It didn't. The illness ate her up slowly from within. Near the end she was just a frail shell. A pale shadow of her former self.

Mum had very thick hair. She looked after it carefully. When she started chemotherapy and her hair thinned out, she cut it all off. She was given a wig. We children said that it didn't matter. That she was just as beautiful anyway. But I remember that she cried.

I never lost hope during the time she was ill. Or perhaps it was rather that it wasn't part of my universe that a life without Mum could exist at all. I made myself turn a blind eye to what was going to happen. Not even when they said that it was inoperable would I give up.

'So she's going to die, is she?' asked my school welfare officer, and clasped her hands together on the table. Looked me in the eye.

'Yeees… Yes, I suppose she is,' I replied.

To this day I find myself hating her for what she said. She was the one who took hope away from me. Nobody should do that. At any rate not to someone who is grieving.

I remember that I prayed to God that she would get her health back. I have never prayed since then.

When we had been given the final diagnosis, Mum said sorry. She cried when she held me in her arms. I shook my head. There was nobody to lay the blame on. Not even me. Despite the fact that I tried. I wasn't enough – not big enough to be able to take the blame. Perhaps that is what makes me most angry and sad. There is no one you can put the blame on. The world is unfair. That has been the hardest lesson for me. I'm still naively hopeful when it comes to justice. Despite the fact that I don't believe in God.

Dad is a doctor. He saw to it that Mum was nursed at home. She and the rest of the family wanted to get away from the hospital. As she got sicker, Dad stuffed bits of paper into the doorbell and we had to brush our teeth with our mouths shut, all so that she wouldn't be disturbed. I remember that I sometimes felt very irritated because her illness controlled our lives. But the anger soon passed. Her life was about to end, mine would continue. There was no reason to deny her this peace.

A nurse came to our house and helped her when she found it harder to manage on her own. I think she hated it. When I was born she had difficulty in walking and then she also had the help of a nurse until she regained her strength. She told us several times how awful she had thought it was.

Mum died on 27 April 1999.

The closest relatives were gathered around the bed where she lay gasping for breath. She had begged for something warm to put on her feet. The blood disappears from the extremities of the body first, like in the winter when it's cold and one doesn't have any gloves on. A weak rattle in her throat, her back arched, sank slowly down and then she was gone. Mummy was dead and I was only 14 years old.

My memory fails me here. Everything has been erased. Mixed up. Only fragments are left, pale images appear and disappear. I cried myself to sleep for a week.

Mum had written a diary for each of us three children. A last greeting that we were given after she had died. It makes me feel secure to have her own words as a reminder of her voice.

At school there was silence. Nobody said anything. They had sent flowers when she was ill but afterwards not a word. This silence made me feel different and excluded. When someone asked an ordinary question about Mum and I told them what had happened almost everyone said, 'Oh, sorry!' Their sympathy made me feel even more out of touch. I found myself getting angry about what they said. Why did they ask me to forgive them? It wasn't their fault. Oh, sorry! Then it seemed there was nothing more to say. It was as though they had turned their backs on me.

I wanted the whole world to stand still, take a breath and let me catch up. It didn't. After a time I just wanted to have someone to tell the whole story to, somebody who would listen. Somebody who didn't belong to the family. I wanted to find that person myself, but found no one. The longing to talk about it disappeared when people sought me out and asked questions. I just wanted to feel close.

Now, for the first time, I have been able to achieve some kind of framework. It took me a year before I could talk about Mum's death. It took even longer before I was able to discuss what had happened with others and share their ideas about grief, but I really want to say: Don't be afraid of seeing grief-stricken people cry. We are not angry at you. We are feeling the loss of someone we love.

I used to see Mum in town after she had died. Someone with a similar hairstyle or clothes. I wanted to scream. Grab on to her and hold her in my arms. Not let go. But I was always wrong and my scream stuck in my throat.

My dreams were filled with her. She came to me at night and promised that everything would be alright again and as usual. And so it was always – until I woke up and opened my eyes. Those mornings I could see no reason to get up.

I never got to know Mum, not as an adult. My brother and sister and I have been deprived of that. Therefore I will never know if I am like Mum, if I behave in the same way as her. I can only get other people to talk about her. Let others tell the story that she should have told.

While I was growing up she was always there. Without exception. I was safe. Secure. The time afterwards was the complete opposite. We recreated a sense of security, a badly needed imitation of what had existed. But not strong, not in the same way.

I got to know Dad through Mum's death. Until then he had only been a father figure. The one who coped with things and was strong, but I didn't really know who he was. The last remains of my concept of the universe fell to pieces when I realized that he too was a human being. That even he could be wrong, and break down. After a time he found himself girlfriends. I still can recoil when I see him with another woman by his side. But I think he needs it. He has to have a chance to be happy too. It's terrible to live alone. Nowadays Dad is my best friend.

Now I've stopped thinking 'if only'. I am a completely different person, of that I'm sure. I'll never know who I would have been if Mum had lived. I would possibly have been 'younger' and not as old as I feel now.

I lost a couple of years of my life when she died. There was no longer any place for childishness. There were other things to think about. How you prepare food and how a washing machine works. We were suddenly minus a person in the family. Everyone had to help each other and I was never a rebellious teenager. Probably never felt the need. I just wanted to hang on. Keep hold of what I had left.

When I think about death I feel on the brink of tears. Fear spreads deep into my soul. If I were to have children I would never let them lose a parent. It would be way beyond what was reasonable. Nobody should have to go through it. Nobody. But one can never have control over everything, can never know. I started to write sometime after she died. Because in the world that I construct in words, I have control. In that world I decide who will live and who will die.

If I shut my eyes I can still hear her voice whispering comfortingly to me. Her warm hand against my cheek and darkness flees away, always. Everything is going to be alright, I think. It has to be. I still have hope.

Lina

*'Now he can fly without a plane because
now he has wings of his own, like the soft,
silky fur of a newborn kitten.'*

Lina was born in 1992.
She was ten years old when she lost her father, Jensa.

It happened so suddenly.

I had been waiting for at least three hours, but he never turned up. I felt my heart beating faster and faster, as if I knew what had happened. It was at midsummer. My little sister and I were sitting out on the steps and I thought I heard a crash. When I was told about it I believed it was a joke, but still I knew it was not.

The policemen who arrived said it so abruptly. Just that he was dead. I asked if it was possible to bring him to life again, but they said it was impossible.

Later on they let me see him. It looked as though he had just fallen asleep and would soon wake up, but he never did. I felt that a great part of my heart was dead. There was a hole inside me that could never be filled again. Without him I can no longer see fairies dancing over the water.

We used to sit down on our jetty in the mornings and watch that misty whiteness. He took a cup of coffee with him and we talked about all sorts of things, like about what we were going to do that day.

All that had gone. All the happiness had gone. I had so many feelings for him, so much to ask him about what he was like when he was young. I had just read his old diaries that I found in a cupboard and written poems to him that I wanted him to read. I think he would have liked them. I felt like the loneliest human being on earth, but glad that I still had Mummy and my sister.

When Daddy disappeared the sky turned dark and silent. Otherwise he was always up there flying his plane when the weather was fine, when birds were singing and the bumblebees humming, as though they knew that we'd be able to watch him fly that day.

I often went with him. The first times I felt sick, but got used to it. When we flew up into the mountains we landed on water close to a rock where we stood and fished for salmon and trout, which we took home and fried, and they were delicious.

It was fun flying among the clouds. Once we saw another plane a bit below us and suddenly it was beside us. It was Daddy's friend. They started talking over the radio, diving and hiding from each other and it was fun. Now the plane has been sold. The man who has bought it is going to try to put it together again. When I grow up I want to learn to fly.

I don't know what happened. The day before, Daddy had tightened all the plane's nuts so that nothing could happen, and he was a very good pilot. He had no life jacket, but he didn't usually have one. He just wanted to finish up the petrol before he landed to fill up with more, and while we were sitting and waiting I thought I heard a crash far out over the water.

Now he can fly without a plane because now he has wings of his own, like the soft, silky fur of a newborn kitten.

The world is not the same as it was before. I felt that I didn't want to live any longer and that I just wanted to disappear. But I managed to survive those hard times.

Now I can also think about happy memories of Daddy. We used to play games and he had just taught my sister and me Monopoly and we played it that last day at our summer cottage. He won all the time of course. We just got bankrupt.

I still sometimes feel as though I'm dragging a load of heavy stones behind me. And I wonder what he thought before everything became silent. I wonder. He probably thought about us!

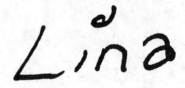

Wilhelm

'The thing I like best is when somebody
sits down with me to have a talk.'

Wilhelm was born in 1986.
He was 14 years old when he lost his father, Jonte.

Myself!

I am 18 and in the middle of taking my driving licence. So far things have not gone that well. I got 51 out of 65 in the theory test and the pass mark was 52, but it is just a matter of trying again. My interests are sport, TV games, boats, cars and other motor vehicles. I am forward-looking and positive, make friends easily and when I have managed to get started on something then I give it all I've got to make it as good as possible. I give a lot of time to my friends at cafés and pubs and my nightlife accelerated when I turned 18. I was born under the sign of Taurus, pretty persistent, and when I have my driving licence I'm going to buy a car and go on a car trip through half of Europe with a friend.

I care about my family and my friends and easily get sad in sympathy with people who are close to me. As long as my family is fine then I am fine.

The time when Dad was ill

It started on a Monday in the spring of 1997, when my dad, Jonte, was in the middle of lunch at his Rotary Club and he suffered a stroke in the left side of his brain. After the ambulance trip to the hospital he went through tests and operations.

He was in hospital for a month or so and then at the Rehabilitation Department, to get back the strength in his legs and arms. After a few months he was able to be at home and go off every day to do his physical training.

During that period we spent a lot of time together. It was good both for me and for Dad. While he was healthy he used to say that he would be home at a certain time, but he used not to be able to keep his promise, which led to me sitting alone at home until late in the evening before he arrived back.

In 1997 I was only 12 and I believed that Dad was the strongest man in the world and could do just about anything.

That changed in the spring and summer of 2000. Dad had such difficulty in focusing his eyes that he went to have them examined. It was a malignant brain tumour that had to be removed as soon as possible so that it would not spread to other parts of his body. After the operation I saw

Dad crying for the first time. It made me feel unsure about whether he would survive or not.

He was at home during the whole of the summer, which was very demanding for Dad and also for us. He had chemotherapy twice a week and was a bit frail for the remainder of his life. He became sensitive to bumps in the ground, loud noises and if one talked too fast. As soon as something disturbed him he got nauseous, which made us anxious.

My life during Dad's illness

I had just started the seventh grade when Dad fell ill, and I played tennis, football, hockey and volleyball. Things went well because I had two parents who could help out by driving me to where I needed to go in the car. We spent every weekend at Dad's house by the sea, were in town during the week and spent the summers at the house that Grandpa purchased in the 1900s. (I have now been bought out of it and instead have my own little house, which I am happy with.)

This life, quite perfect as it was, disintegrated when Dad fell ill.

I began to understand how ill Dad was when we watched a film about cancer and death at school. My life had also taken a turn for the worse and I had to accept responsibility far too soon. I skipped a couple of years, and no longer had any childish discussions with Mum. We talked about houses and everything we had to do. Of course I am still her child, but nowadays I am more like a friend who lives with her. Luckily I had decent friends. One girl helped me with everything, from doing the cooking to doing my homework. I only knew her as a classmate at the time when she helped me out by starting to talk to me. The thing I like best is when somebody sits down with me to have a talk.

Dad got sicker and my marks got worse, not that I had been among the best in the class, but I sank from a clear pass to landing among the worst after half my time in the eighth grade. Dad progressed deeper into the illness and in the end my friends did not dare to ask how I was. Sometimes I did not have the energy to go to school. It was not much fun. We wanted Dad to be at home and have Home Care. We thought that was nicer, but sometimes he could not cope, and nor could we.

In the ninth grade I had a very good teacher and was on my way up. But in October Dad passed away and that caused a long downswing for me again.

There was the funeral and a dinner at the SAS Radisson Hotel. A lot of people grieved over Dad and that felt strengthening, but also difficult because there are a lot of them who I have not seen since. Sometimes I pass Dad's friends who frequently used to visit us at home, but who often do not greet me any longer.

My life turned into a rollercoaster. One moment in a good mood, the next too tired to lift a finger, because I have been so sad or felt generally disturbed. I cared less and less about school and was hardly there. But then the teacher started making demands on me after she had asked Mum if it was 'okay to put pressure on Wilhelm' and I got through the ninth grade without a single failure, except in handicrafts.

Mum, my sister (who is Mum's daughter, 11 years older than me, and who always defends me even if I am in the wrong) and I made a trip to the Canary Islands for a break after Dad's death, and it was one of the best New Years that I have ever experienced. The three of us travelled to China for the Sports Week holiday and that was also a very nice trip.

When we were back home again I tried to live normally and my friends started behaving as they usually did, but sometimes it hurt. When they talked about Father's Day – it was really a bit grim. And when I hear and see my contemporaries talking to or hugging their fathers, or wrestling with them, it makes me ache. A friend's father died six months before mine and the two of us got on fairly well together and were able to talk about it.

The whole of the first year at my sixth form college, for students aiming at a career in uniform, went very well in fact. To attend it you have to renounce xenophobia, racism, bullying, truancy, drugs, vandalism and violence. I am doing a sociology programme, with courses in survival, kayaking and fly-fishing. But after the first year I had plans for a year off. As was the case with my class teacher in the ninth grade, my headmaster had been my mentor and I missed him when he went to Afghanistan on a UN mission. But the Swedish language teacher took over his role. I have always tried to find a grown-up because I need to be helped along and now I have promised my class teacher and my games teacher to return after the summer holidays. I got through the second year with a pass in almost all subjects, largely thanks to my policy of not having a girlfriend before I turn 18. It is incredibly nice not to have a steady relationship.

Dad and me

Dad is with me all the time. I have a cross around my neck that reminds me of him, that I was given after my confirmation. It feels as though he has saved me many times from being injured and I have an unmistakeable example. Only a few hours after his death I was playing in a match, because I knew it was what he would have wanted me to do. I was tackled from behind and flew head first into the sideboards. But I was unscathed. I also have very good memories from the period of illness, because even though Dad was on his deathbed, he made plans for us, for a month or a year ahead. When he was at his worst he planned that we would buy the house we are now living in. The purchase of the house and confirmation are the best things that have happened to me since Dad died.

It was the wife of the vicar who I talked to and who helped me to be accepted at a confirmation camp when she realized that it was urgent. There was a very kind atmosphere at the camp, a lot of people who cared about each other, and I have never experienced such an atmosphere anywhere else. The people taking part and the parish were all super. The vicar was quite wonderful.

When I think about Dad now I think about his considerateness and I miss the social aspect. He was hypersocial, hypernice, liked by everyone, and he was considerate to everyone.

Tove

*'We wanted to see the tree where Daddy
hanged himself. Sten and I climbed up
and carved Daddy's name into the tree.'*

Tove was born in 1987.
When she was 12 years old she lost her father, Örjan.
(Tove's younger brother, Sten, tells his story on page 39.)

I love board games. No one else in my family does, but that Friday Daddy and I played Scrabble. I was happy, because of being able to play, and because I won and Daddy thought that I was clever.

Later on in the evening the series *Worlds Apart* was cancelled. Instead there was ice-hockey that Daddy, my younger brother, Sten, and I watched. I had difficulty in falling asleep that evening because I had a pain in my jaw. Daddy lay and patted my head until I fell asleep and promised to ring the dentist the next day.

On Saturday morning when I got up there was a note in the kitchen:

> Woke up early.
>
> I have gone down to the sea for a while.
>
> Örjan

I spring-cleaned my room while Mummy cleaned the house. As the morning wore on I started to wonder where Daddy was, but Mummy was calm, so I did not think about it any more. But half an hour or so later the police rang and wondered if we owned a Mitsubishi and then Mummy got worried. She rang some of our best friends, and they came over. Granny and Grandad arrived too. Everybody was worried, and Mummy and I watched *101 Dalmatians*. Sten watched ice-hockey. Mummy and the others went out to the chairs in the garden. I was deeply engrossed in the film so I stayed where I was.

Soon after, Mummy came in. She called Sten down, lit a candle and sat down on the sofa between Sten and me. Then she said, 'Now I'm going to tell you the hardest thing I will ever have to tell you: Daddy is dead. He chose it himself.' Sten and I were silent at first. I did not believe it was true. Then I remember that I screamed, did not cry but screamed. I just wanted to faint, felt sick, wanted the time to pass. Sten and I asked what had happened. I could not understand that he had chosen suicide; it was quite simply impossible.

After a while we started ringing round everybody. To relatives and our closest friends, Mummy's and Daddy's as well as mine and Sten's.

We went outside and sat in the garden. I drank a vitamin C drink nonstop and Grandad drove off and bought ready-made meat soup, which we heated up but forgot to dilute. Flowers started arriving and people dropped in. It was good to feel that people cared, that they were thinking about us.

My father's brother, father and great uncle arrived during the night. It was incredibly good that they came so quickly. When we said hello to them it was the first time I cried with tears in my eyes.

In the morning there was the thanksgiving service and the pastor announced that Daddy was dead. My friends came to it and I was so happy about that. Several of Mummy and Daddy's friends were there too, and afterwards we went home and had snacks.

My friend came around in the afternoon. We did not do much, but she was there, she cared, and she sat with me while my godfather patted my head till I fell asleep. That night I slept like a log.

We wanted to see the tree where Daddy hanged himself, so me, Sten, Mummy, our relatives and close friends drove there. It was a lovely area. First we walked along a stream in a dark, rather gruesome forest. Then we arrived at a glade where there were deciduous trees instead of evergreens.

The trees there were not so close together, and the tree was beautiful, divided into two trunks that wound themselves round each other. You could see the marks of the rope, and that felt weird. We couldn't really understand it properly. Sten and I climbed up and carved Daddy's name into the tree and put roses at the foot of it. We walked around there for a while.

It was nice to feel that Daddy died in such a lovely place. In the middle of the forest, with a cup of coffee.

We saw Daddy the day after. I was scared beforehand, because I thought that I would see a wrinkled, icy-cold person. When we came into the mortuary he was lying there. He had no wounds or marks. He was a little paler than usual, and rather cold, but otherwise it just looked as though he was asleep. Sten and I closed Daddy's eyes, and then we stood there, crying a bit and holding his hands. It felt as though we had only been there for five minutes, but it was quite a lot longer. It was good to see with my own eyes that he was really dead.

Sten and I started school again four days after Daddy's death. Mummy thought it was much too soon, but I felt that I had to get on with my ordinary daily life. My friends behaved as usual, and that was nice. They let me sit with my friends instead of in the place that the teacher had given me, and we lit a candle in the classroom every day until the funeral.

Mummy's friend helped us to buy clothes for the funeral. It was tiring to go in and out of shops, but fun to be given nice clothes. I had on a white flowery dress.

There was always someone sleeping over at our house, and that was a very good thing. We felt secure with people around us.

On the day of the funeral we drove up to the church and did the flower decorations on the coffin with the help of a florist. It turned out very well. We constructed a landscape with shells, blue flowers, reeds and boats, moss and stones, which symbolized the sea and the nature reserve on our island. There were masses of flowers.

The church was full of people at the funeral. There was a lot of music, and that was nice, but I was nervous when we were supposed to walk up to the front. Everyone started crying when we stood there by the coffin. Everyone in the church went up one by one and laid flowers on the coffin and then just about everyone came and greeted us, and I felt as though I was being stared at.

The coffin was carried out and lowered into the grave. I do not remember anything about that, but then we ate sandwiches and cake. People made speeches but we children went outside and played. It felt good that the funeral was over, but it was hard. Only two weeks had passed since Daddy died, and there was an eternity left of my life.

We talked a lot about Daddy the whole of the summer and autumn. We wrote diaries for the days just before and just after he died, and those diaries helped a lot, partly because we were able to go through everything and partly because it is very good to have them now. Everything is grey and blurred from those days, but with the help of the diaries I can remember exactly what I thought, felt and saw. I wrote down things that were typical of Daddy, for example that he chewed toothpicks while he was trying to stop taking snuff, that he had holes in his underpants, words and expressions that he used and memories of daily life. I still write things in that diary, when I think about Daddy more than usual.

I wrote this on 6 May 1999: 'I don't feel very much, I have not really understood yet. I believe that he will return but I miss him. Now I am looking at a photo and it feels as though he is looking at me. He has his toothpick in his mouth. Blue jersey over a greyish-white shirt and a blue casual jacket. I feel empty and I feel sick from thinking that only two weeks have passed of the many decades that are left!'

Sometimes months pass without my thinking about him. I think about him mostly when I meet his relatives or read old diaries and at more important celebrations. The day of his death is not so important. I almost forgot it last year, until a friend reminded me. But I can feel a bit sad when I see children doing things with their fathers. Planning something, arguing about something, or just saying goodnight. Then I want him to be here with me.

I am not afraid of talking to people who were there about how things are for me, but also about how they felt and reacted. With new people the conversation often turns to parents, and I have to tell them that he is dead. Many say 'sorry' straight away. Perhaps they are afraid that I will start to cry.

Obviously it differs from person to person, but I like people to carry on with their questions, how he died and why.

I remember Daddy as being secure, strong and protective. Good at telling stories and very popular with other children, because he made up games that were fun. The image of Daddy is changing as I get to know more about what he was really like. He never showed Sten and me that he was depressed.

Now afterwards I have understood that he felt rather weak at times, but I think that it was a good thing that he kept such a lot about how he felt from us. I had a big, strong, happy father, even if the grown-ups perhaps knew better than that. If he had lived I would have wanted him to tell us more, as we grew older. But I do not believe that you need to know everything about your parents. I am glad that I have the picture that I have of Daddy, and that I do not remember him as a depressed, weak person.

On 24 April 2002 I wrote in my diary: 'Three years have passed already! In the autumn we are going to move to the city to live at Olle's, and I am going to stay with Granny and Grandad during the ninth grade. It really feels like fun, and it's really cool at school. I do not often think about Daddy, sometimes, but seldom…My life without Daddy is good but it would have been better with him is how one can sum up the past year.'

Mummy met Olle about a year and a half after Daddy died and they got married three years later. I like Olle. He did not come along and think that he was going to be my father. He is there, as a person one can go to, a bonus father. Sometimes it feels upsetting that Mummy met a new husband. I want Mummy always to belong to Daddy. But, even if you do not believe it when the worst thing that can happen to a child has just happened, life does carry on.

Sammie

'After Daddy died I started doing the things that he used to do at home. I pick up the spiders that come into the house. Mummy finds them scary.'

Sammie was born in 1992.
When he was seven years old he lost his father, Micke.

Monday 21 February 2000 changed my life. That day something happened that I thought couldn't happen to me. My father Micke died. He had a heart attack. It took only a few seconds to end Daddy's life. He had gone and nothing was as usual. Nothing was fun. It has taken several years for me to be able to feel happy inside again.

I can still get very angry because he is dead. Then I sometimes smash my fist on the table and throw myself on to my bed and cry. It is worst at Christmas when we are at Daddy's parents' house.

The police arrived in the evening, at Daddy's parents' home first and then at our home, and they told us what had happened. I was already in bed asleep. Mummy's parents and brothers and sisters came and stayed with us all night.

Mummy woke me the next morning and what she told me and my little brother was almost like a ghost story. At that moment everything seemed to disappear. What Mummy told us was so awful that I could hardly breathe.

At first I didn't understand a thing. Everything just sort of went round and round in my mind. After a couple of minutes it was as though everything turned dark, as though the whole world went out.

It happened the first day of the sports holiday. The days right after that were hard. Everybody rang and they were all very sad and we were given masses of flowers.

When I started school again the work felt tiring. I often started crying, but my friends came and comforted me. It was hard that nobody else in my class knew what it was like to lose a parent. But some of them had lost a grandparent.

At home it often happened that when one person started crying, everyone else in the family started crying too. It felt a bit safer at home than anywhere else. Not as lonely. There was always somebody to talk to.

Daddy had driven to work in the lorry thousands of times and had always come back home. He worked away one week and was at home one week, so it was easy to pretend that he was only working a little longer than usual and that he would soon come home. The visit to the mortuary was awful. It was a horrible feeling to see Daddy lying there pale and cold and to understand that he was far away from any kind of life. But if we hadn't gone and seen him in his coffin, then perhaps we might not have believed it even now. I felt sorry for my little sister who didn't understand anything at all.

At the funeral everything was quiet and it felt as though my whole life ended. When Daddy wasn't there everything was much harder. Things that I used to do with Daddy felt hard. What I loved most was to be with Daddy, so now I feel a bit lonely. Daddy used to be out driving his lorry and I sometimes went with him. And the whole family used to spend time in the forest cutting down trees and sawing and chopping them up for our wood boiler. We talked about everything. About his job, about us, about school. He taught me to do carpentry, carve, ride a bike and be a good person.

We used to go out in town and thought of all sorts of things to do. We enjoyed fishing, both winter and summer, and we used to take a picnic basket with us. We listened to music. He was a nice, kind, pleasant person, quite tanned, thin-haired and with a moustache.

After Daddy died I started doing the things that he used to do at home. I check that the doors are locked before we go to bed. I pick up the spiders that come into the house. Mummy finds them scary and before it was always Daddy who carried them outside.

When we are at the grave all my memories jump out at me and it feels weird to think that I will never ever be able to meet Daddy again. Daddy is always inside me in my heart. I hope he can see me. I miss Daddy so much that it is impossible to find words…

Mummy has put together an album about the whole of Daddy's life from when he was a little boy. She has written a lot and stuck in lots of photos and everything that has been in the newspapers about when Daddy fell ill and drove off the road in his lorry. It is on the bookshelf in the living room and I sometimes take it up to my room and look at it.

I worry that something might happen to Mummy too. If she is out I usually ring and ask if everything is okay because if anything happens to her then there's no point in living, I sometimes think.

Mummy has a new husband now. It's a bit difficult, but a good thing anyway.

I think that it is inappropriate to refer to a stepfather as a 'pretend father' or a 'fake dad'. I got angry when one of my friends called Benny my pretend father. Benny is Benny and Daddy is for ever my Micke.

With best regards,

Sammie

Jennifer

'Then the women told me what had happened.
"Your mother is not alive any more," they said.'

Jennifer was born in 1986.
She was 12 years old when she lost her mother, Annika.

My whole life changed in a split second. Something I had never believed I would ever lose didn't exist any longer. I was 12 years old when Mummy was taken from me. Nothing would ever be the same again. It is impossible to describe what it feels like to stand there alone, afraid, forsaken, bewildered and lost, and not know where to go or what is going to happen.

Monday 8 March

Woken by Mummy as usual at about seven. Breakfast in bed as usual, and toothbrush with toothpaste on it on the washbasin, as always.

When I come out into the hall Mummy is standing by the chest of drawers and ringing to say that she will not be coming in to work today. Daddy is sitting in the kitchen reading the newspaper. The atmosphere is tense and unpleasant. Daddy is going to stay at home too. He wants to talk to Mummy. I leave for school earlier than usual. Can't bear to be at home. Mummy comes with me to the door. I am cross and I glare at her. I am so angry at Mummy and Daddy because they always have to quarrel. We say 'goodbye' (for the last time). Mummy's expression was so sad when she shut the door.

The whole of Monday I had a strange feeling in my stomach. I felt in my bones that something was going to happen. I couldn't concentrate in class and had forgotten my glasses when I hurried away from home. I knew that they were going to have a row and could not bear it. My anger drove me to school. I just wanted to get away, although I really did not want to leave. I wanted to stay with Mummy. Wanted to protect her from Daddy.

At lunchbreak I thought of going home. But had such a strong feeling that I shouldn't, despite the fact that I ought to have fetched my glasses. I just knew that something was wrong.

During the last lesson the class was supposed to go and borrow books. I had a book with me from home, so I stayed at school. The others went to the library. I stayed sitting at the back of the classroom with the book open at the first page. But did not read a word. I sat in my own thoughts, certain that something had happened. I looked out of the window on my right. Outside it seemed to be windy. It was slushy too, and most of the snow had melted. I tried to read. The lump in my stomach had not dissolved.

Time passed until it was 2.40 p.m. I shut the book. Looked at the clock again, thought of going home, but perhaps it was best to wait for our teacher.

Five minutes later she came into the classroom, out of breath and red in the face, as if she had been running. It was clear from the expression on her face that something was wrong. She crouched down beside me, said that two people wanted to talk to me, said that they would be arriving at any moment now and that I was to wait in the classroom. She patted me on the knee and went out again.

The lump in my stomach grew and I squirmed on my chair. It felt like forever before they arrived. It was two women who introduced themselves by their first names. We went and sat down in a little room. One of them thought that we should switch on the radio. Why on earth? I thought. My teacher switched on Radio Match. It played Ricky Martin. Then the women told me what had happened. 'Your mother is not alive any more,' they said.

It just grows dark. An enormous wave inside me is trying to reach my head and something bursts. Like putting a needle against a balloon. Bang. Tears stream from my eyes. Gush out. I have pins and needles in my body. My tears started flowing before they said it. I already knew what had happened.

The women talked to me, but I did not listen, everything around me vanished and there was nothing. Only the tears existed, and the lump in my stomach that grew bigger and bigger. I had the creeps; everything just wanted to overflow out of me. My teacher held me tightly.

When I had calmed down I no longer knew what had happened. I did not understand anything. Didn't know if what was being said was real.

They asked if I had a granny or anyone else I could go to. I wanted to go to my best friend. I had to go with the women to their office. Had to sit in a room, alone. It was small, and they left the door open. There was a window and an armchair. I sat down in the armchair and looked out of the window. Cried quietly. I do not know what I thought.

One of the women came in to me and said that they had not got hold of my friend's parents, so I would have to be driven to my teacher's home. She lived out in the country.

The whole evening was just total chaos. The police arrived out there, as well as a psychologist and a pastor. Masses of questions were asked the whole time. I couldn't cope. Everything was going round in my mind. I felt so small, so insignificant, so helpless and lost.

My teacher sat with me until I fell asleep. But I only pretended to sleep. I wanted to be alone and cry. It was only far into the night that I fell asleep. Still crying.

The next day I was allowed to my best friend's home and talk on the telephone to my brothers, for the first time since they had left for a long trip in India. They were going to take the first plane home.

The time that followed continued to be chaos. We lived at my oldest brother's, in his two-room flat, he, my younger big brother and I.

The days passed and I was supposed to return to school. I wanted to. I missed my friends. A pastor had talked to the class about what had happened. So everyone knew about it when I went back. On the day of my return there was a little memorial ceremony in church for Mummy, just for my class and the class that I had attended the year before. I remember that I cried, but my friends were there with me. That was nice.

We went back to school afterwards. Our teacher provided snacks for us. It was almost as usual. A lot of them avoided me and hardly said anything while others talked to me as though nothing had happened. It was fun to be back.

Our teacher had bought a present for me. Watercolours and a pad. Painting was the thing I liked best. But I associated it with Mummy, because I always used to paint pictures for her. So I let it just lie there.

My oldest brother became my guardian. It was a long time before I was allowed to talk to Daddy again. I had missed him so much. My brothers and I went to visit him in prison a couple of times. It was upsetting to go there, and we started to lose contact slowly. He never rang any more.

My brothers and I moved back home to our flat. I was about to start secondary school and was afraid and nervous. Nobody there knew how things were. About my background. Imagine if someone asked, 'What's your mother's name, and what job does she do?'

The class that I was in for seventh grade was very good. It did not take long before everyone knew about my situation and everyone seemed to accept it alright. They treated me like everyone else, and that was nice. I got a best friend and she became like a sister. I told her everything. And she told me about her life, which had not been all that easy either. She was my new soulmate.

My youngest brother soon met a girl. I did not like that of course because he was my brother. I did not want him to be taken away from me, but he soon moved to her place. After a year or so they got married. I didn't go to their wedding.

Then only my oldest brother and I were left. But soon he met a girl too. I moved back and forth between my brothers until I made the mistake of having a New Year party at my oldest brother's. Then I had to move to my other brother and his wife for ever.

Three years passed and I was due to start sixth form college. Same anxiety and worries as before secondary school. I would be losing the class where we had such good community spirit and where everyone was so close to everyone else. Now I would be starting in a new class again, where nobody knew anything. There was no certainty that my friend and I would end up in the same class either. Then I would be totally alone and vulnerable. But in the summer holidays I had a language course abroad with her to look forward to.

The first year in sixth form college was hell. My friend and I did not get into the same class, but luckily she was allowed to change to my class.

There was nobody we liked except one person. The others kept away. We three were left alone together. That meant that I missed my time at secondary school even more. I was terribly unhappy and felt worse and worse.

My brother and sister-in-law whose home I was living at were worried about me and contacted the psychologist I had been to after Mummy's death. I started to go to him again. It turned out that I was suffering from a depression and that I was on my way deeper and deeper into it – depression caused by Mummy's death. It was expected and now it had arrived. I got tired easily, had no energy for anything other than being with my friends. They kept my head above the surface. But it soon felt as if there was no hope left... Then I met a guy. He became my lifesaver and gave me the love I had been missing for such a long time. I said nothing to start with. Didn't dare. I had lost my trust. He might leave me as Mummy and Daddy had done. I really did not want to lose him. In the end he begged me to open up to him and I did, something I had not done with anyone for a long time. We met every day. I was in love and my whole life circled around him. He kept me alive. But one day everything changed again. We started arguing. Argued every day. It affected us both terribly, but me most of all because I thought I couldn't survive without him.

He did not want us to meet as often as we had. I could not cope with being separated from him and started cutting my wrists. I hit myself on the head so that I got big bumps. I threatened. Wanted to show him what would happen if he left me. I went there at night. Sat outside his window. Rang the bell in the middle of the night. Locked myself into his bathroom and cut myself while he stood outside and yelled and banged on the door. Everything got completely out of control. In the end I could not leave his place of my own accord. My brother had to come and fetch me.

Things carried on that way for a few months until the situation became intolerable. I asked for help, I thought not only for my own sake but also for my boyfriend's. My brother, who was my guardian, and I talked to a doctor at the Child Psychiatry Unit. My psychologist was there too. It was decided that I was to go to a Special Approved Home. But it would take time. So what should we do until I could be admitted?

We drove to the psychiatric ward. My brothers came too. They said that we were only going to see if I would consider staying there for a weekend. But when I went on to the ward I just wanted to go home. The atmosphere was unbearable. It looked so old. A long, long corridor with brown, worn wooden doors that were shut. I suspected that a lot of them were locked. The air was dry and stuffy. I got the creeps just being there. I spoke with a quite young guy on the staff who did not seem to understand that I did not want to stay there. When we had finished talking my brothers said that I had to stay there. That it was the best thing to do. I was furious, felt panicky, screamed and knocked over a plant standing on a table. I rushed through the corridor knocking over plants, hitting out, kicking and screaming. I hate being locked in. I did not want them to leave me in a place like that.

I calmed down but was still shaken. One of the staff tried to talk to me. I wanted to go home. Rang my brothers several times. Nagged, cried and begged them to fetch me. But it was useless. The staff came with tranquillizers and sleeping pills. I did not want to sleep. I was up all night reading magazines in my room. Fell asleep from pure exhaustion around dawn. Woke late in the morning and rang my brother who came and fetched me. He did not really want me to be there either.

The week after I was to go away to the Special Approved Home. I took as much with me as I could: my computer, an armchair, a table and my stereo. The room I was given was on the upper floor. It had a window looking out on to the garden, a wooden floor and dark-blue wallpaper. Quite a large room, but with a low ceiling, and it was gloomy. It was going to be my home for three months. I really did not want to be there.

The Special Approved Home was out in the country and had Iceland ponies. I rode in the forest every day, but felt worse and worse. Rang my brother as soon as I had a chance and begged him to fetch me. He refused, but said that he would visit me in a week's time.

In the end I had had enough. Just wanted to go home. The feeling was stronger than anything else. I walked five or six kilometres in the direction of the city and hitched the last bit with an old man who was very hard of hearing. He let me off near a kiosk and I thanked him for the ride.

Went in and bought a refill for my mobile so that I could ring my brother and say that I had escaped. Just then I saw one of the staff sitting in a car outside. He had seen me but stayed there, waiting. I ignored him and walked a little way away. Rang my brother, who tried to get me to go back. But I just wanted to go home. The man from the Special Approved Home drove up and stopped beside me. I was driven back. Didn't say a word either on the way or for the rest of the evening. I was just angry.

The next day I learnt that the staff had cancelled my appointment with the psychologist. I was furious and said that they couldn't do that. That I wanted to see him. But the staff considered that it was not a good idea for me to go into the city after what had happened.

I cried in a rage, knocked things about and in the kitchen I found a knife. It was blunt but I cut my own cheeks and rushed out of the house. Ran the same way towards the city as I had walked the day before. If my brother did not want to fetch me, then I would have to get home by myself. The sun was blazing down so it was very hot. I had on a thick sweater but did not bother to take it off. I walked for a good distance before a car stopped with four 25-year-old blokes in it. They were on their way to Stockholm to watch a football match. I did not say very much during the journey. I still had the knife hidden in the arm of my sweater. We were approaching the city centre and I hopped out. Near the City Library I threw the knife in a bin and stood in a queue waiting for the bus. I was on my way to school to find my boyfriend. Who else could I turn to?

My lenses were very dry from all the crying. I could hardly see and my eyes hurt a lot.

At school one of my friends was sitting outside a classroom. She fetched our other friend from the classroom and they scolded me because I had cut my face and escaped. She was probably mostly scared. I went to the staffroom and used the telephone. Rang my psychologist. He came and fetched me. My brother came too. We drove to the social welfare office and everything that had happened was discussed. The social welfare officer could see no other solution than to drive me out to the Special Approved Home again. I got up, said that they might as well just shoot me at once, walked out of the room and slammed the door behind me with a bang.

I went straight to my boyfriend. We hugged each other and I told him that I had escaped. He was glad to see me. He had missed me. We have been through such an incredible lot together. I am very lucky to have met somebody like him, who has stood by me the whole time even though he was almost about to crack up too.

My brother rang and said there was a chance that I could get temporary lodgings in the city that very same evening and that felt a lot better.

I soon became friends with a girl who was living there and three months passed quickly. Then they arranged for me to move to a one-room flat in a Support Home. But I am going to look around for a flat of my own, one that I have chosen myself.

My contact with Dad isn't terribly good. It is up and down. He comes and visits me when he is on leave over the weekend. Most often we sit at home at my place and talk a bit. He usually helps me with things in my flat and we cook together sometimes. We meet every other time he is on leave and go and have coffee with my big brother, his partner and their daughter. He sleeps at a youth hostel and on Sunday afternoons he takes the bus back to the prison again. It is upsetting for both of us when he has to go back there. I want him to stay of course. That is probably what he wants too… I think he will be released in a year's time and hope that we will have more contact then. Hope that one day I will have him back in my life. That he will be 'Daddy' again.

My oldest brother is the most important person for me. I will always see him as a 'Dad' because that is what he was for five years of my life. And now I have become an aunt too.

I still see the psychologist and have had depression for two years, but I am slowly on my way out of it. I have shown my strong will these past years and want to be healthy. So it is not impossible.

It is true that Mummy will never come back to this life. But she is inside me. She's still here with me anyway, every day.

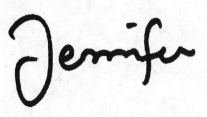

Robert

"'How did he die? If it's okay to ask?'"
"He drank himself to death. An alcoholic.
Chose booze instead of us.'"

Robert was born in 1983.
He was nine years old when he lost his father, Morgan.

The open-air café was bursting at the seams with people. The sun was shining, the trees were singing and the heavens seemed to be tinted with a wash of watercolour blue.

'What does your father do then?' she asks, blowing her fringe out of her face so that I can see her brown eyes.

'He's dead,' I say.

'Oh shit, sorry.'

'You don't need to say sorry, it wasn't your fault.'

My father died in December 1992. It was just after the first Sunday in Advent. The previous Friday we had lit the first candle on the Advent candlestick and had been given cinnamon biscuits in the classroom.

I was nine years old and never really understood properly why he disappeared. Just that he was dead and gone for ever. I had hoped for a white Christmas. Instead it was as black as night.

Gothenburg is a beautiful city, especially when clad in the colours of spring. The sun's rays have enticed the buds to burst into greenery and summer is on its way, if it is not already here.

'Do you miss him?' she wonders.

'I don't know. I really don't know.'

'But you must miss your father.'

'I missed him then. Just when he had died and a few years afterwards. But since then – I don't know. I'm angry mostly. Bitter perhaps. If one can possibly be that towards someone who is dead.'

She shrugs her shoulders. How could she know? Her father is alive.

Two weeks after Dad's death I was back in the classroom. A lonely boy at a school desk. My teacher gave me a blue notebook. 'Write,' she said. 'Draw, pour out everything that you can't say to anyone.'

Two schooldays later I had created something. I had used that dumb, thorny feeling of unreality that had invaded me, used that feeling and made something out of it. It did not feel better. But more real.

About a month before Dad went into hospital I had a terrible dream. I dreamt that I got up in the middle of the night and opened the door to Mum and Dad's bedroom. And there lay Dad, his breath rattling and blood oozing from the corner of his mouth. Now I am not sure that it was a dream. The same haziness lay over the dream as over the whole situation the day he died.

Mum and her sister return from the hospital and I am standing in the hall and understand that something is wrong. Several relatives are at our home as support. Dad is going to have an operation, something is not right. Mum and my aunt come in through the front door, Mum with tearful eyes and an empty smile, everyone looks at them, waits for what they are going to say, but nothing is said, they just shake their heads slightly and I hear my cousin give a scream. Dad is dead. The hall fills up and is so full of people, but I become empty, so incredibly empty.

We have just been served the coffee that we ordered.

'How did he die? If it's okay for me to ask?'

'Yeah sure, it's okay.'

She looks at me. Fiddles a little with the coffee cup in front of her. Clearly she is curious.

If somebody finds out that one's parent is dead, there is nothing that they want to know more than what happened. Most people do not dare to ask straight out, since they are afraid that they might reopen old wounds. But much more is necessary for me to remember and feel pain. Much more than that is required.

'He drank himself to death. An alcoholic. Chose booze instead of us.'

'Oh shit.'

'Oh well, it doesn't matter now. It is only that – that there is so much more that I have understood afterwards. Why certain things happened – why he talked in a funny way sometimes and what that special smell was that his clothes reeked of.'

When I turned 12 my notebook was published. My private fragments of text and the pictures that I had drawn. It was Mum who sent it to a publisher's. I remember that I appeared on the Morning News on TV4, in a youth programme. And in an evening paper.

After a while letters started arriving for me from other children who had also lost their fathers. But I did not reply. There was nobody who could really understand anyway.

My small siblings came to me if they had problems or if they wondered about something. I took on that protective role of my own accord. The role that Dad should have had. That he would still have had if he had not drunk himself to death.

Can one feel bitter towards somebody who is dead?

'He betrayed me. He betrayed me and the family.'

I am not angry when I say this to her. It sounds more like a cold statement of fact. Because it is true. He committed the ultimate betrayal towards his son. He disappeared. He left me on my own. Left his family on their own. And that is a betrayal that is hard to forgive.

She looks at me. I see that she is trying to understand. She is trying but cannot.

'Are you afraid of becoming like him?'

I nod.

'Parents are not what one is going to become, they are examples of what one can become,' she says, lighting a cigarette.

And of course she is right.

The year I was due to turn 16 the whole family moved to a small town in the south of Sweden that mostly has pizzerias and hairdressers lining its narrow streets. Quite a radical change from Stockholm's noisy concrete jungle. But I learnt to feel at home, despite the fact that I began to lose contact with my friends in Stockholm as time passed.

In the new town my memories began to fade. From having been my father, the one who knew everything, who made the decisions, the one who had suddenly died, he became just a memory. Nobody spoke about him. Nothing reminded me of him. The few photos where he is present are standing on the bookshelf in our living room, it is true, but they are just standing there collecting dust.

Mum has met somebody new. I suppose it was just a question of time. He is an alcoholic too. Who could have guessed? I have read that certain people are drawn to such individuals. Such a pity that it just happens to be our mother. But we have survived in any case.

After sixth form college I worked as a trainee on a local newspaper to qualify for a course in journalism. That is where I am now. Tramping the streets, back and forth, up and down. With my hands in my pockets or else sitting on a bench somewhere, writing in my little notebook. And here, where I am, I do not need anyone. I am strong enough to manage without a father figure or role model. Because that is what I have done since I was nine years old. I survived, but I really hope, sincerely, that nobody else should ever have to go through anything similar. Nobody should have to survive alone.

I feel how he is fading away. How he is in fact dying in reality. And I do not know what I should feel about it. Indifference is not a pretty trait. Not for me either – I have sworn never to betray my future children, never to die and leave them and never to fall down drunk in the hall with blood running from my forehead not knowing where I am – particularly not if my greatest admirer and eldest son is standing in the bedroom doorway trembling and crying with fright.

I hope you are having a nice time wherever you are, Dad.

I am having a truly excellent time.

But not everything has been said. Not really.

When I was 16 Mum told me that the father that I knew, who brought me up, who I had grieved over and missed, was not my biological father. How do you react to something like that? I was dumbstruck, mainly. With tears beginning to drip from her eyes, Mum told me how she had been unfaithful, and that was how I was conceived. Dad, the one who died, was never told anything.

My biological father wanted to have me, and create a life with my mother, but she drew away from him and continued to live her life with the man she had chosen. The one who became my father. The one who died.

I have met my biological father. He is a nice man. We sometimes give each other a ring and then we usually say to one another: 'We should meet more often.' But he is far too involved in his own life, like me. He has other children and I have college. And there is the distance. A distance that will always be there. Geographically and emotionally. We do not know each other. Not really.

After that I had three father figures. One who is a part of my life as Mum's new partner, who I do not see as a father, one who is dead, who I did not have any blood ties with, and one who is alive but not really a part of my life.

My own father does as well as he can. He is there. I see characteristics in him that I have too. He wants the best for me. But we will never be father and son. And perhaps that was never the intention.

She raises her eyebrows and says, 'You mean that you really have three fathers?'

I look into her beautiful eyes. They are sparkling. Sparkling with wonder and curiosity. And I understand her. Things are not always what they seem to be at first.

'And I have one mother,' I say and smile. 'I am a Mummy's boy. And that is just as well.'

She smiles back and puts out her cigarette, pressing it hard against the ashtray, with an almost confused expression in her eyes. 'Don't you feel cheated?'

'I don't know,' I say. 'I live with it in some way. The past, what happened before, is a part of me now. There is no reason to accuse anyone. Especially not my mother. She is the only fixed point I have had in my life.'

'But…'

She seems to be doubtful, does not really seem to grasp what I have told her.

'How are you handling all this? What has happened and so on, I mean?'

People around us have started to put on their jackets and the wind is sending wisps of hair like a veil over her face.

'I write. That is my therapy. Letters are my tools. They soothe and are creative. They are there for me.'

She nods. It is starting to get cold. The spring sun is treacherous. It warms you one minute and the next moment it takes cover behind a cloud and seems to suffer from performance anxiety.

We leave. An older couple are walking hand in hand in front of us. They seem happy. A tram bell clangs. She lights another cigarette, but has to cup her hands and huddle up with her back to the wind before it lights up.

In some way it is beautiful.

I write but what I write is not about Dad or about myself. I try sometimes but it is hard. So incredibly hard. I write down some clumsy sentences now and then, about what I have pushed aside for such a long time. Stare at them and rub them out. Those letters were unable to explain or tell the story. They were just letters, hardly symbols for feelings. Not mine anyway. It gets so soulless when I reach the very core of the problem: that I am living a life without knowing who I really am. So dry and cold. And it is precisely this that frightens me, since that is exactly how it feels.

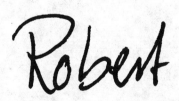

Norah

*'In Swedish lessons we got a sentence with
"Mummy" in it. The teacher changed it to
"Daddy". I think that was kind.'*

Norah was born in 1993.
She was three years old when she lost her mother, Christina.
(Norah's big sister, Julia, tells her story on page 35.)

It feels strange not to have a mother. I do not know what she was like or anything. But she is in my heart.

One thing I remember is when I was little and peed in my pants all the time. Mummy and Daddy thought that they would teach me to go to the lavatory and Mummy asked me (when I was sitting on the toilet): 'Can you do some "tinkle tinkle" for me?'

I remember that she gave me yoghurt once. And I've got an old teddy bear that I was given by Mummy when I was three years old. She had been given it by Granny when she was three.

I feel quite alright without Mummy, but when somebody in my class says, 'I would never be able to live without my mother,' then I say, 'I have no mother, but I feel fine.' Then they say, 'Oh, sorry, we forgot about you.' Then I get angry, because they should not forget things like that.

We do not talk about Mummy very much and I feel a bit that we do not need to do it. But when we are doing the cleaning at home then I wish she was here with us. We have so many things to keep in order, and I've seen in old films that our house used to be very tidy – I have Daddy to help me. He is the one who mends my bow, rows the boat and drives the scooter. And cooks food like Mummy's.

When we were doing nouns and adjectives in Swedish lessons we got a sentence with 'Mummy' in it. The teacher changed it to 'Daddy'. When somebody asked why she just said, 'It's because Norah hasn't got a mother.' I think that was kind.

When I was little we watched the TV programmes *Bananas in Pyjamas*, *Postman Pat*, *Play School* and *Super Mutant Ninja Turtles*. I asked Daddy if he thought that Mummy would have liked *The Lord of the Rings*. 'Yes of course,' he said, 'Mummy was a film-lover too.'

Darling Mummy, it feels as if you have escaped out into space and can't find your way back home again. I miss you very much! Can't you come back? Mummy, is there a heaven? If there is then I want to come and visit you. Have you met God? Can I have his autograph?

If you have escaped, then I don't know why you did it. Perhaps you were sad, scared or angry? But I will find you, when I die.

Love,
Norah

Kalle

*'Mummy couldn't wake Daddy. Not even the doctor
could wake Daddy. It wasn't anyone's fault.'*

Kalle was born in 2001.
He was one year old when he lost his father, Mårten.

Kalle is his nickname. He is too little to be able to decide whether he wants his real name and face to appear in a book, but Kalle's family is letting us include his story. Ken Chesterson, who is a child psychologist, wrote down what happened exactly as Kalle's mother told it. The psychologist has read the story to Kalle time after time. He nods, corrects, fills in bits or shakes his head and loses interest if there's something wrong somewhere. At every visit he wants them to read 'the book about Daddy':

Once upon a time there was a boy called Kalle. He lived with his mummy and daddy in a house in a town. One day they visited Granny and Grandad in another town. When they came home, Kalle sat with Daddy who read *Alfie Atkins* to him while they waited for the children's programme on TV. Then Daddy got tired and lay down on his bed.

Mummy suddenly got extremely worried. Daddy was very ill. He started to shiver and shake in a strange way. You could hear in Mummy's voice that she was very frightened. Kalle got very frightened too, 'and sad'. (This was one of Kalle's additions, when the psychologist read the story again after ten months, when Kalle was two years old.)

Kalle's heart beat fast, fast. Mummy ran to the telephone and rang the ambulance. She blew air into Daddy's mouth to make him breathe again. Then she pressed his chest to restart his heart.

Kalle patted Daddy's leg to make him wake up. Daddy didn't wake up. Then Kalle patted him harder. Daddy lay still. Then Kalle patted even harder – but it didn't help. Kalle wanted Daddy to wake up and be as usual. Kalle did everything he could and was very clever but he couldn't wake Daddy. Mummy couldn't wake Daddy. Daddy was so ill that he died. It wasn't anyone's fault. Not Kalle's, not Mummy's, and not Daddy's either.

Kalle was very frightened and ran round the bed because he wanted to be close to Mummy. He wanted Mummy to wake Daddy, but she couldn't.

The doorbell rang and Mummy ran and opened the door. It was two women who had come with the ambulance. Mummy lifted Kalle up and handed him to one of the women. Kalle was afraid that Mummy would lie down on the bed too and not wake up.

Then Grandma and Grandpa arrived.

First Daddy was taken away to hospital in an ambulance. Then Mummy and Grandma left in another ambulance. Then Kalle went with Grandpa by car to the hospital. Granny and Grandad arrived too.

At the hospital everyone was so sad because not even the doctor could wake Daddy. He was dead.

Kalle thought that they must be able to wake Daddy. He got sad and angry.

It was the middle of the night but Kalle couldn't sleep.

He had to go home with Grandma and Grandpa and stay there for several days. He was worried about Mummy. He was afraid that she would lie down on the bed too and not wake up, that she would get as ill as Daddy, and that she would die.

Kalle tried to play but he couldn't. Sometimes he was sad for a long, long time. He called Daddy but Daddy didn't come. Then he got very angry. Daddy had to come! But Daddy didn't come, anyhow.

Kalle longed for Daddy. Daddy used to go with him to the sandpit and dig and build. Kalle and Daddy used to play football. And Kalle used to snuggle up to Daddy on the sofa while Daddy read to him. *Alfie Atkins.*

Kalle wanted Daddy to come and play with him. Play in the sandpit, play football, read *Alfie Atkins.*

But Daddy didn't come back. Kalle got sad sometimes and angry sometimes. Now there was only Kalle and Mummy. Kalle sometimes stayed with Grandma and Grandpa and sometimes with Mummy at Granny and Grandad's.

Then it was the funeral. Daddy lay in a coffin with a lid on. First the lid was open so that you could see Daddy, then it was shut. There were lots of flowers in the church.

Kalle saw that lots of people were crying. Kalle didn't want Mummy to be sad. But she was. She couldn't help it. Then the coffin was put into a hole in the ground. Lots of people threw a flower into the hole, Kalle too.

Kalle and Mummy started to live at home. Kalle went to nursery school again.

One day, Kalle went with Granny and Grandad to the cemetery. To Daddy's grave with the headstone. Kalle carried two candles. He was happy and walked as fast as he could to Daddy's grave. The lighted candles were beautiful. Kalle had a little toy horse with him.

Kalle tried to get Daddy to come up out of the grave. It didn't work. Kalle tried again but Daddy didn't come out. It didn't work because Daddy was dead. His heart had stopped beating. Then you can never breathe again or move or open your eyes or talk. You're dead and you can't change that.

Kalle got very angry. When they got back to the car he threw his horse on the ground and stamped on it. Kalle was really very sad because he longed for Daddy and wanted him to come back. It was such fun when Daddy was alive. Everyone was much happier and Kalle and Daddy had so much fun: the sandpit, football, *Alfie Atkins*…

Kalle wanted Daddy to come back – he called Daddy but he didn't come. It wasn't Kalle's fault. Kalle did all he could to get Daddy back, but nobody could make Daddy come back, not even Mummy, or Granny and Grandad or the doctor. Daddy would certainly come back if only he could. But he couldn't. Kalle was sad sometimes and angry sometimes, because he longed for Daddy and wanted to have fun with Daddy.

Now lots and lots of days have passed since Daddy was alive. Kalle gets sad sometimes and angry sometimes but the moods pass more quickly. And Kalle will never forget Daddy. (Kalle smiles now when he hears these words in the book. He has just turned three.)

Sara

'I am throwing myself out into the unknown, 70,000
fathoms. You have to live and see what happens!'

Sara was born in 1984.
She was three years old when she lost her father, Christer.

Who will comfort Toffle? was the story Daddy read to me on our last evening together. The last evening before he disappeared, out and away from my life.

When I was three years old Daddy took his life, and my life and my future were changed for ever.

Mummy and I felt very bad after Daddy's death, as was to be expected.

Mummy got pains in her joints. It was there her grief settled. One vivid memory I have from that time was of one morning when I was supposed to be going off to playschool, but there was no Mummy up making the breakfast. She was lying in bed with pains in her body. I felt fear then because things were not as usual.

It often happened that we were angry and yelled at each other. Me, a little child who could probably not really understand or did not want to accept what had happened, and a sad mother with no patience.

The island where I lived for my first 12 years was where Daddy had lived as a child. Grandpa's divorced wife, Daddy's mother, was left behind on the mainland. Daddy probably never got over the separation from his mother and it was there that the seed was sown that led to his taking his own life in the end.

Daddy was a poet and author, and very poor. He had temporary jobs here and there to enable him to get by, just about.

In the summers he returned to the place where he had grown up and he lived in a spartan way in a beach hut, on blueberry soup and cheap Co-op bread, while he wrote and thought about life. He later also met my mother on the beach.

He mended his shoes until there was nothing left of them and his shirts had so many holes that in the end people gave him their old clothes.

I have been told that he was full of witty comments and very entertaining because of his original way of thinking. He had a capacity that was sometimes troublesome – that my nearest and dearest often say that I have inherited – of seeing and inconsiderately pointing out people's weaknesses.

And he was probably not very kind. It could be difficult to defend oneself against his quick-witted psychological attacks, which happened when he was not feeling terribly well.

During my childhood, when I thought about Daddy, I felt hurt and inadequate. Were I, his own child, and my mother not reasons enough for him to want to live? As time passed I learnt quite simply that we were not enough for him.

At school I often felt different. Perhaps it was because I had to meet one of childhood's bigger challenges so early on: losing a parent.

I often played with boys and was seldom part of a gang of girls, but I did not really feel at home anywhere. It feels as though the path of my life since Daddy died took a turning away from most people's. No ordinary life with two parents. Instead I was allowed to go everywhere with Mummy and was often in adult company. That brought with it masses of interests that were slightly odd for a child of my age, like cross-stitch embroidery. But this gave me a much better and closer relationship with Mummy too, and I do not know how I would have managed without it. We have gone through a lot together, Mummy and I, since I became a bit more than just a little child.

When I turned 12 Mummy decided that we would leave the island. And go not just anywhere either. We were going to move to Italy. We had been there a lot since I was eight and we had friends there. But anyway, it was awful, I thought, but I did not have much to say in the matter. So we sold my childhood home and drove down to Tuscany with all our goods and chattels. I went to a private teacher and learnt Italian, and in September I attended an Italian school. I did not like it at all. Swedish schools were heaven by comparison.

Luckily, although it was also rather a disappointment, we did not get the house we had been promised, and before Mummy succeeded in finding something else after a desperate search, she got ill and we went back to the island, but ended up in a town after our little adventure. There I immediately got a warm welcome at school. In a town you could be yourself more easily than in the country, without it necessarily meaning that you were alone, because there were quite simply more people there. The result of our move was good in the end. I felt very happy in the town and nowadays it is probably there that I feel most at home.

When I was 14 Mummy met a new partner. It was a very trying time. Mummy had not had a relationship since Daddy. I had grown up without men and to have to share her now and feel that she did not need me so much was very hard. At the same time I was ashamed of wanting to have Mummy to myself.

But the change was also for the better. When I was 16 Mummy moved out to his place in the country, and I lived alone in the town. I was at school there of course. I had to start paying bills and being responsible for my child allowance early on. I bought my own food and took my economic responsibility seriously. I compared prices and got absorbed by it.

Nowadays I feel that it was mostly positive. Of course, sometimes it got too much and I rang Mummy and cried, but what you don't die of makes you stronger, as a friend often says.

The only negative thing is that I sometimes notice among friends and people of my own age that I have had to grow up sooner, and I sometimes feel a certain irritation, perhaps envy, towards those who have not needed to.

I sometimes feel that Daddy's death has made me rather careful emotionally. That means that I do not like laying the responsibility for my happiness in life in others' hands. I rely mostly on myself. My trust has probably been injured.

This carefulness has made me into a good listener, I think: attentive to how my fellow humans are feeling. Nobody will ever be able to take me by surprise again, is what my subconscious seems to want to say.

At the same time I find people fun and interesting. It is possible that my perpetual desire to discover new dimensions in people I meet is based on my need to understand the human psyche. Perhaps I need to understand in order to be able to forgive Daddy. But it is hard to be sure of how one works oneself. (Or anyone else, for that matter.)

Nowadays I do not think about Daddy especially often. I am far too busy living. But when I think about him it is in connection with how I am myself and why. It is a bit like searching for one's genes, seeing similarities and wondering who he was and who I am.

Sometimes I wonder what sort of a person I would have been if I had been allowed to grow up with him, and known what he was like as a person. If we had had our own relationship and I had been able to get to know him.

When I was little I cried now and then and was clearly angry at him, but that is a long time ago now.

Time has healed my wounds, and I am quite satisfied now with my life and with who I am. That is how it feels now a year after I left school and after I have lived abroad again. It has given me so much and taught me to dare to trust that things will turn out well. Thinking about the future gives me a feeling of excitement and the joy of life! You have to live and see what happens! In the immediate future I am going to pick grapes at a vineyard in Italy.

Now I am throwing myself out into the unknown, 70,000 fathoms…

Sara

Marcus

*'We celebrate New Year together, and go shopping
to try and have some fun despite it all.'*

Marcus was born in 1989.
He was 14 years old when he lost his mother, Jeanne and his father, Claus.
(Marcus's twin sister, Charlotte, tells her story on page 183.)

My family and I travelled to Khao Lak in Thailand on 16 December 2004 to celebrate Christmas. Mum's sister and her family were staying two hotels away. We lazed about together, sunbathing, swimming and shopping.

On Christmas Eve our hotel ran a Christmas theme with a very beautiful Thai buffet and we all gave each other our Christmas presents in my and Charlotte's room since it was the biggest. On Christmas Day we went out snorkelling and diving. It was wonderful, almost the best I have ever done. In the evening we relaxed and had dinner near the hotel that we stayed at two years ago. And we went to bed early because we were going diving again the next day.

The next morning Dad said that there had been a slight tremor during the night. The chairs had moved. Just a slight, little earthquake, he thought.

Mum and Dad were going to do their test for a diving certificate at about midday and they had swotted a lot. They were rather nervous. Lotti and I thought they were boring and I lay down on the bed again to finish the film we had started watching on Christmas Eve. *The Day After Tomorrow.* About an enormous wave. Quite weird that it was just that film.

Mum, Dad and Lotti went down to the beach.

While I am lying there watching the film the electricity is cut off. There is a sudden sound like thunder and heavy rain, as if a giant thunderstorm is on its way. I look out of the window – and see a wave that must be 15 metres high! I get a bit of a shock and think I am dreaming. I see bungalows being swept away, and cars, and people lying bleeding, and I understand nothing. Grab the room key and want to run down to the beach, but all the paths and steps have gone. Get very worried for Mum, Dad and Lotti. See people floating in the water and start crying. A Swedish man asks if I know where my family is. We have to get to higher ground. It is chaos. Wounded people everywhere. The road has been washed away. Everybody is just screaming. Nobody understands a thing.

My aunt's family comes running. They have seen it, thought 'shit' and rushed straight to our hotel to see how things are with us. Everybody starts crying. My cousins aged ten and six are terribly frightened, and we are too.

They let us jump into the boot of a car full of wounded people. The man driving it shoots off at 130 kilometres per hour. We follow the coast, see the destruction and arrive after a while at a hospital. People are having operations on the lawn. There are a lot of tourists, quite a lot of Swedes. We become a little gang who intend to keep together. Everyone is very sad. We have to drive 50 metres in a big bus to a hangar, really a badminton court.

There we lie down on the concrete floor, on millimetre-thin mattresses with silk sheets. The hall fills up, dusk falls and it is evening. We have still heard nothing about Mum and Dad and Lotti. We are given water all the time. Thai people come along with enormous amounts of food. Apart from that it is disgusting, with blockages in the drains and lavatories.

I manage to fall asleep despite the bright strip lighting on the ceiling. Get woken up by sirens and flashing blue lights. We are given rice and omelettes again. I walk back to the hospital with two girls, or women – one is missing one of her daughters, the other her whole family. We look around. I still get flashbacks to the horrible sight of one man who was covered in blood and had lots of wounds.

That day they start laying out bodies where we are. We have to check the bodies, see if there is anyone we recognize. My uncle has his mobile and everyone is allowed to use it. I ring my girlfriend in Sweden.

On the third evening my other aunt rings from Stockholm. She tells me that my sister is alive!

Lotti has been taken care of by a Thai family. On their computer she has been able to email her best friend in Sweden. But Lotti has not known for several days that I am alive.

We have to leave the hangar. New waves might come, new earthquakes. We are not safe here and are driven to a place where they issue passports and where different countries have aid commissions. We talk to the Swedish consul, fill in forms again about those we have lost. The Thai people said the whole time that they were alive and were at some hospital. They had mixed up the documents. At the consulate we are given some fries to eat. They taste very nice.

During our last days in Thailand we sleep at an international school. While we are sitting in the back of the lorry on the way there, Lotti succeeds in contacting my uncle's mobile. The lorries stop so that I can hear her. Our lorry drives straight to Lotti. We find her sitting on a sofa with crutches and sores all over her. We all cry for quite a long time then. All the Swedes are very happy for our sake. Also the two women who have been a bit like extra mothers for me during the first few days.

We celebrate New Year together, and go shopping to try and have some fun despite it all. The day after, we are going home.

It felt very strange flying home without Mum and Dad but there was really not much else we could do. Five people back at home were ready to fly out there and look for our parents. At the airport in Stockholm we had to register the people who were not with us on the trip home. Relatives, my girlfriend, a friend and Lotti's friend were waiting for us. It was very upsetting to meet them. We all went to my aunt's.

It was only at the beginning of term that we went back to our own house, and the hardest thing of all was to see all the photos of Mum and Dad.

A little care rota was set up for the first few months. My aunt, Dad's brother's wife and a workmate of Mum's took turns at sleeping over at our place to look after us.

The school held a meeting about our situation, about how we were feeling and so on. Teachers and friends gathered around us and asked loads of questions. We had a minute of silence in the class. The Minister of Education came to our school when the whole country had a minute of silence, and an evening newspaper wanted to do an interview with us, but we did not have the energy for that. It was nice anyway to go to school, though I mostly just sat there thinking about Mum and Dad.

My aunt received an email in the middle of January from a Thai woman who thought she had found Mum at a temple in Khao Lak. Mum had a ring inscribed 'Jeanne and Claus, 1985', the year that they were married. It was such a shock although I had begun to have a feeling that they would not be coming back. The woman who wrote was not 100 per cent sure that it was Mum, so I kept on hoping and trying not to think about it too much.

Two months later, when we arrive home from school, our aunt is sitting on the sofa crying. Mum has been identified. At first I do not believe that it is true. Feel totally empty. But I go to school the day after because I want to have something normal, and it feels good to be at school.

Two days later Dad has been identified too. Now everything is sort of wrecked, desperate, even though I carry on at school, though without being able to focus on work. It is starting to feel strange there too. During the first weeks everyone had been very kind. Now my friends have already stopped talking about it. I feel a bit abnormal going around feeling sad when everyone else is happy.

When the bodies arrived home the whole of Mum's and Dad's families were at the airbase to receive them. The other families were there to collect relatives too. Seven bodies arrived. We were the only ones to have lost two people.

The hearses formed a ring. They played beautiful music. The coffins were covered with Swedish flags. We were allowed to go forward and lay our flowers on them. It was very unreal. I just cried and cried. It all felt like shit. When everyone was ready some soldiers sang a bit more. The hearses drove away one by one and we went home.

We started to meet a pastor and plan the funeral. I was very nervous. My sister and I had never been to a funeral before. It was very strange that the first one was our parents'.

Five hundred people came to the church. People stood way out in the entrance. Everyone from Mum's work was there and many, many people from our school. We played lots of songs that Mum and Dad liked. Afterwards it was just us relatives and we took it very easy. It feels nice to have them here in Sweden anyway, in a cemetery near us.

We moved when we knew that they had been found. Lotti and I wanted to stay in our own area close to our friends, and when we had just got back home some of our neighbours, friends of Mum and Dad, said that they would really like to take care of us. That family has two boys aged 15 and 13, who we have spent a lot of time with, and after a couple of months we moved in with them.

It felt very strange to take everything from one's own room, leave one's own home and go to a new family with other rules. We were given our own rooms and we have our own things, but during the first period I felt like a lodger and did not know how to behave. Felt that I forced myself on to their family and tried to take up as little space as possible. But I have learnt how to fit in. Now I am more a part of my new family. We really have a lot of fun together. The boys and I have a great time riding mopeds and playing ping-pong together and we call each other brothers. The rules changed a lot, of course. I had been out pretty late, partying and drinking and here I was not allowed to do that. But they are wonderful to us and I do as they say.

We still have the house. It is empty and I go there to cut the grass and so on. But we are inclined to sell it and have approached an estate agent. At first I really wanted to keep it, but now I do not feel that strongly. I do not think that I would want to live there with all the memories when I am grown-up. And the house itself will still be there whatever happens, if I want to see it.

Sometimes I feel alright, sometimes I feel unhappy, even very unhappy. When my ex-girlfriend stopped seeing me I wrote very strange text messages about not wanting to live any longer. I had to go to the Child Psychiatry Unit then and they helped me with lots of advice about looking forwards not backwards. I have probably thought the whole time that Mum and Dad want us to live as happily as possible and that we should make the most of our lives.

The thing that has helped me the most otherwise is the Children's Social Rights organization BRIS. We are in a group of eight who were in Thailand. It is comforting to talk to others in the same situation. We give each other support and have quite a lot of fun there. I did not even know what BRIS was and did not want to go there at all, but I do not regret it.

In the ninth grade I had a nice teacher. I had been in her class for three years. She and the other teachers helped me a lot. We sat and talked, and they let me use my phone when I wanted, and if I had no energy to stay in the lesson I could just go out and get a breath of fresh air. They even helped me with my homework at school all spring, so I never needed to do any homework at home.

I have started sixth form college and have new classmates. In the beginning, when we talked about our parents, where they work and so on, it was hard. Nobody knew what had happened to me. Not until I entered my profile on a youth site, where you chat. Now perhaps they say, 'You have to make something of your life, not just give up' and so on. But they mostly seem to think that I do not want to talk and they do not want to force themselves on me in my struggle with grief.

Dad was at home during his last year. He had sold pharmaceuticals factories and wanted a change of career. He and Mum were going to open a hotel together and he was busy planning for that.

When I sit by the grave and talk to them I think that they are probably having a pretty good time up there too. Nowadays it helps me sometimes to look at photos of them and think about all the fun things we have done, and how we were able to sit and talk, and how they always supported me. And yes, how they loved me.

Young people who complain about their parents should be glad that they have any. When I visit friends who sit down to dinner with their whole family I think they are so lucky and so fortunate while my sister and I are all alone. But I am also more grateful now, for what so many people give me. And I take each day as it comes.

The sights from the tsunami only come to mind if I think about them. But I can get panicky when there is thunder.

We flew back to Thailand in June and managed to have a ceremony with a pastor. It was a good thing but hard. It was during the monsoon period, windy with enormous waves, but I conquered my fear of the water. I went down on the beach and stood in the water again. A bit scared, but I did it.

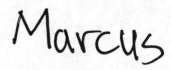

Charlotte

'I'm fine but something has happened. A giant wave came and took away Mummy, Marcus and Daddy.'

Charlotte was born in 1989.
She was 14 when she lost her parents, Jeanne and Claus, and wrote about it shortly afterwards.
(Charlotte's twin brother, Marcus, tells his story on page 175.)

It felt so empty flying home from Phuket without Mum and Dad, before we knew anything and were just wondering what had happened to them.

I do not understand why Dad did not run towards higher ground when he saw the wave. And what happened to Mum that stopped her from surviving?

On 26 December 2004 a great darkness fell over the world. Why on earth was I allowed to live, when so many children in the world died?

Boxing Day in Khao Lak

The whole family had a gorgeous breakfast. Mum had gone out early to keep sunbeds for us. Marcus wanted to stay in the room and watch the film from Christmas Eve to the end. He promised to come down when it was over.

Mum, Dad and I are lying on the sunbeds. Mum is reading her diving magazine. I rub sun lotion all over me. Dad is looking out to sea in a strange way. Mum and I look up and see the water disappear leaving all the fish on the sand. A lot of islands appear. We see children running out to help the fish back into the water, so that they will not die. Dad wants me to fetch the camera from the hotel so that we can film the water disappearing. I am too lazy. Dad is going to fetch it himself, but first he and Mum have a little argument. Dad thinks that the water is drawing out. Mum and I shriek, 'It's coming in.'

'Calm down, of course it isn't coming in,' says Dad on his way up towards the hotel. I have not seen him since.

Mum and I see the wave approaching. We pick up our stuff and run. Mum runs away ahead of me. I hear her voice: 'For goodness' sake run, Charlotte! Whatever happens I will always love you.' I have not seen her since. She disappears without bothering to check whether I am behind her. I run in panic, upwards, as far as I can. Get to a flight of steps where there is chaos, in front of me and behind me. A small child is standing by the steps crying. The mother has left the child alone.

I am holding tightly on to the stair rail when the wave roars in over the whole of Khao Lak. I feel the wave rolling over me and pulling away the rail. I follow the wave out to sea and in again, several times. Under the surface I swallow gulps of salty water when I try to get air and feel that I will not survive if I do not come up to the surface. In the end I can take deep breaths. With my eyes closed. I am hanging in something, a tree? The roof of a house? I do not look. The thing I am hanging in snaps or breaks and I am pulled out to sea again, out and in. After perhaps seven minutes I open my eyes and notice that I have landed up by the hotel and see masses of people lying there, blood spurting out everywhere. I am crying and shouting 'Help!' A man helps me to my feet. 'Where do you come from?' asks a woman. A Swede. She calms me, gives me a towel, asks which hotel I am staying at, the room number, what my name is, what family I have, how old I am, the names of Mum, Dad and my brother. She says that it is all going to be alright. I say that I am in a lot of pain and that I am very frightened. My foot is blueish-purple and crooked. I cannot stand on it. Since I am in such pain the Swedish woman says that a couple of Thai women want to send me to the hospital in an ambulance. I do not want to go away from the woman, but have no choice. They carry me on a stretcher and drive off with me.

Then I see my aunt coming running with my cousins and I do all I can to get the driver to stop. Yell, wave, knock on the windowpane, but there is chaos again. Water has flowed over the road. I get very frightened. The Thai women who are with me say that everyone has to get up into the hills because there may be more waves on the way. The man who is driving stops and runs away uphill without helping me.

I creep and hop up the hill. My foot is starting to turn brown. A family live up there and they give me water and a few clothes. The woman helps me to scrape off the blood with some leaves. I discover a Thai woman here who worked in the reception at our hotel and she knows English. After seven hours the danger is over. We climb back down the hill. The Thai woman helps me. That is much better than being alone.

We leave for the hospital. The woman translates for me. There they wash my body and my hair, fix all the wounds and bandage my foot properly. Then we go to her home. Her family give me clothes, a lot of food and flip flops. At night I sleep with her in her bed.

On the second evening the woman's brother asks if I want to send an email to anyone. I write something like this to my friend: 'Hi! How are you? I'm fine but something has happened. A giant wave came and took away Mummy, Marcus and Daddy. I am staying with a Thai family and don't know how to get home. Have no mobile, money or passport and think I lost everything else in the wave. Love you, sweetie. Hope to see you soon. Kisses from Lotti.'

People helped me to look for my brother and our parents. On the third day a car came to take me to some place in Phuket. I thanked the family for letting me stay there and for all the money I had been given. When the man in the car dropped me off I was helped by a lot of other people. There were telephones here and there. I was given help with the national prefix and rang my friend (it was late at night in Sweden). She cried and was very shocked. The whole of my family had received my email.

She was the one who told me that Marcus was alive and safe with my aunt's family. 'What, is he?' is all I said. It was very odd that somebody at home could know that. She told me the number of my uncle's mobile, but the conversation was broken off before the last digit. When I rang again her telephone was off. When I at last got hold of the number I only got through to the voice box. I flew in a helicopter to Phuket's airport with the Thai Minister of Transport. They gave me lunch at the airport and let me ring. This time my uncle answered! He almost started crying. 'Charlotte, are you alive? God, I've been so afraid.'

We were only ten minutes away from each other by car.

When I saw Marcus I started crying. Marcus hugged me tightly. My aunt hugged me. I rang my friends and said 'Now I'm with my brother, and it's wonderful.'

We flew home with my aunt's family. After two weeks we got to know that they might have found Mum. I thought alive. It was the opposite. They were going to ring at the weekend with the exact information. We waited and waited and waited. For two months.

It was Mum they had found.

The evening after, we learnt that they had found Dad. I thought alive, but unfortunately it was the opposite, that is, dead. Cannot understand that what has happened has happened. Neither Mum nor Dad was injured or old and they had no illnesses. It is so bloody awful.

I was very ill when we got home. But there was a lot of grief and stress in it as well. My aunt got in touch with our school. They were going to have a minute's silence, but I did not want to be there, or at all the talking afterwards. My two closest friends were going to tell my story to the class, how I was feeling and that I did not want the others to come up to me and ask too much. I wanted to go to school. Of course it was the ninth grade and very important. My two friends did not leave me on my own for one single moment at school and were a great support. They knew everything and were able to explain that I did not always have the energy or strength to go to school, that I wanted sometimes only to cry, that I could not cope with lessons some days, and that my work was sometimes in rather late.

I have chosen catering college, the right choice for me, and I am very interested. Mum always wanted me to learn to cook, like she could, so that we could have a nice time together in the kitchen. But now she is not here to see what I am learning. I could do a lot of things with Mum, buy clothes and dare to say things and never be afraid of making mistakes. Just take baking. I did that every day at home, but do not really dare now. Here we have another type of stove, gas, with live flames, which I am not used to, and I find it hard to ask for help. Mum and Dad helped us all the time.

Mum was the kindest person in the world and put everyone in a good mood, but I suppose everybody says that about their mothers. Dad was sweet. We played cards a lot. They did everything for us, gave us what we wanted, one cannot understand that they could just disappear. Why them? We were having such a wonderful time in Thailand with our pleasant lunch places on the beach. Later we used to shower the salt off ourselves, change to somewhat tidier clothes and walk around looking at things in Khao Lak. Find a nice restaurant with good food for the evening, and sit and play card games in the hotel room.

Now I am living here with some other people, without Mum and Dad.

It is a good thing that there are people who want to look after us, but I cannot say that I am really happy here and it will probably never get much better either. I am the only girl with three boys who have each other and their mopeds. I mostly sit at my computer upstairs in my room. They think they see far too little of me. But I get sad easily, or angry and sulky and start arguing with people. Leave me in peace, I think, and find it very difficult to talk about it. It is easier with friends. I often go to cafés with my girl friends.

Last winter the social services came to our home to interview Marcus and me. To talk about what possibilities there were. We wanted to stay living close to our own house where we have lived for almost our whole lives. It had been suggested that we should live with either Mum's or Dad's relatives. Our neighbours who were good friends of the family, who only lived a few houses away from ours, had immediately said that they wanted to look after us. I had been out with their oldest son and Marcus had often been at their place because he was friends with their youngest son. Now I sometimes call them 'brother' and they call me 'sis'.

Meeting Dad's relatives feels awkward without Dad. Dad and his brothers and parents were very close. I feel so sorry for Grandma and Grandpa, who have lost their boy.

My friend attends the same sixth form college as me, in another class. We do not meet so often any more, but she is still close. I have two new friends in my class, who know what I have been through. I got a boy-friend when I came home from Thailand, but dumped him and messed around with other boys when I was feeling at my worst. I regret it, because he really gave me warmth and it feels empty without him. My ex and I are now good friends, and I really trust his mother and can talk about emotions and how I am feeling with her.

I attend a Children's Social Rights group. There we can really talk about everything. We tell each other what it was like, and cry, and then the others know why. We turn back the clock – I write long letters to Mum and Dad and we talk and write about what might happen in the future. It is interesting to know how the others in the group are feeling and what is happening to them.

'How will I even dare to take a shower?' was what I thought during the time immediately afterwards. To see water, be under the surface, sit in a boat – it all frightened me. But when a friend came with me to my new family's country cottage in the archepelago I dared to jump in and dive for hours.

It was a good thing to be able to return to Thailand in June with Marcus, our aunt and uncle and Maria, who I am living with now. But on the way there I got panicky. Regretted it and just wanted to get out of the plane: think if something similar were to happen again!

Why I was the one who was allowed to live is something I have thought about a lot. And come to the conclusion that it was a question of luck. We could not do anything. Mum and Dad had bad luck. My brother and I were lucky.